Jesus Heals

Jesus Heals

By Allison Gingras

Our Sunday Visitor
Huntington, Indiana

Nihil Obstat
Msgr. Michael Heintz, Ph.D.
Censor Librorum

Imprimatur
✠ Kevin C. Rhoades
Bishop of Fort Wayne-South Bend
December 2, 2024

The *Nihil Obstat* and *Imprimatur* are official declarations that a book is free from doctrinal or moral error. It is not implied that those who have granted the *Nihil Obstat* and *Imprimatur* agree with the contents, opinions, or statements expressed.

30 29 28 27 26 25   2 3 4 5 6 7 8 9

Our Sunday Visitor Publishing Division
Our Sunday Visitor, Inc.
200 Noll Plaza
Huntington, IN 46750
www.osv.com
1-800-348-2440

ISBN: 978-1-63966-203-6 (Inventory No. T2897)
1. RELIGION—Christian Living—Women's Interests.
2. RELIGION—Christian Living—Devotional Journal.
3. RELIGION—Christianity—Catholic.

eISBN: 978-1-63966-204-3

Cover design: Tyler Ottinger
Cover art: AdobeStock
Interior design: Amanda Falk
Interior art: AdobeStock images

PRINTED IN THE UNITED STATES OF AMERICA

To my fantabulous family — Deacon Kevin, Ian, Adam, Abi, and Faithy! A special thanks to my patient and insightful editor, Mary Beth. Thank you for believing in me!

Contents

Introduction

And Jesus went on from there and passed along the Sea of Galilee. And he went up on the mountain, and sat down there. And great crowds came to him, bringing with them the lame, the maimed, the blind, the mute, and many others, and they put them at his feet, and he healed them, so that the throng wondered, when they saw the mute speaking, the maimed whole, the lame walking, and the blind seeing; and they glorified the God of Israel.

— *Matthew 15:29–31*

I have a deep desire for immortality. This has led to an unhealthy obsession with my health. Living with various chronic conditions first fueled my preoccupation with my own health and mortality. Thankfully, this eventually led me to learn more about the healing power of Jesus. I pored over the miraculous healings in the Scriptures, trying to uncover the secret to a long life; instead, I discovered Jesus' healings concerned matters far beyond anyone's physical wellbeing. Ironically, Jesus' healings *do* involve immortality, but not as I thought I wanted it. Jesus' entire life — every teaching, miracle, and action — illuminates the way to true immortality: eternal life with the Blessed Trinity in heaven.

Paradoxically, as I learned about Jesus' healings, I realized that the more I cling to this world and my earthly body, the more I end up stuck on a path that actually leads to death. See, the truth is, regardless of how long we live, we will all still end up, well, dead. The only true immortality is the heavenly option offered by laying down our will, picking up our cross, and following Christ. "If any man would come after me, let him deny himself and take up his cross and follow me. For whoever would save his life will lose it; and whoever loses his life for my sake and the gospel's will save it. For what does it profit a man, to gain the whole world and forfeit his life? For what can a man give in return for his life?" (Mk 8:34–37).

Jesus healed a lot of people during his earthly ministry. Yet those healings weren't fancy magic tricks to show off his divinity. True, he did heal in part to demonstrate his divinity, but even that was to help people recognize that the true miracle he offered was a share in his inheritance of heaven and the reward of eternal life. The Divine Physician provides a prescription for human frailty, and that is the virtuous life of hope, wholeness, and peace this world simply cannot give. The *Catechism of the Catholic Church* summarizes the role of Jesus' healings this way:

> Moved by so much suffering Christ not only allows himself to be touched by the sick, but he makes their miseries his own: "He took our infirmities and bore our diseases." But he did not heal all the sick. His healings were signs of the coming of the Kingdom of God. They announced a more radical healing: the victory over sin and death through his Passover. On the cross Christ took upon himself the whole weight of evil and took away the "sin of the world," of which illness is only a consequence. By his passion and death on the cross Christ has given a new meaning to suffering: it can henceforth configure us to him and unite us with his redemptive Passion. (1505)

I'm still a bit obsessed with my health, and I am working through that pesky desire for immortality with my spiritual director; however, in learning about Jesus' healings, I've come to understand so much about embracing the design God has for our bodies, our lives, and, most importantly, our souls. I look forward to sharing these lessons and Jesus' remarkable stories of healing with you throughout this book!

So why did Jesus perform healings during his life on earth? Every miracle healing that we read about in Scripture reveals something about Jesus and teaches us about who he is and who we are in him. Fr. Richard Gribble, CSC, explains it in his book *Who Do You Say that I Am? Exploring the Question of Christ*:

> Possibly the most visible role of Jesus as portrayed in the Gospels is that of miracle worker. In his first publicly recorded statement in the synagogue of his hometown of Nazareth, Jesus proclaimed, The Spirit of the Lord is upon me, because he has anointed me to bring good news to the poor. He has sent me to proclaim release to the captives and recovery of sight to the blind, to let the oppressed go free, to proclaim the year of the Lord's favor. (Luke 4:18–19) Jesus brought the good news through proclamations, but also through the curing of the destitute — lepers (Mark 1:40–45), the crazed Legion (Mark 5:1–20), and the woman with a hemorrhage (Mark 5:25–34) — and raising the dead to life (Luke 7:11–17; John 11:1–44). By such action he brought good news to others. Not only did he restore the physical sight of the blind, like Bartimaeus (Mark 10:46–52), but possibly more importantly cured the spiritual blindness that was present with many, including the man born blind (John 9:1–41). Additionally, Jesus's ability to control the weather (e.g., Mark 4:35–41) marked him as a miracle worker in a very profound way.

One of the Old Testament names for God is *Jehovah-Rapha*, which means the Lord who heals. *Rapha* means to mend, repair, or restore something to its normal or useful state. Reading through the Old Testament, we discover evidence of the Lord performing physical (see 2 Kgs 5:1–19), emotional (Ps 34:18), mental (Dn 4:34), and spiritual (Ps 103:2–3) healings. Each healing has one main purpose: to bring the person healed, and those who witness the healing, closer to God. Jesus, who is the fullness of God's revelation, takes these healings to a whole new level as we read throughout the New Testament. His healings do remove sickness and restore physical health, but they fulfill other important roles as well, which I have come to understand more deeply after delving into numerous biblical commentaries and theological works. This list merely scratches the surface of all the blessings and revelations that Jesus' healings proclaim:

- Through his healings, Jesus fulfilled prophecies, like this one from the Prophet Isaiah: "The Spirit of the Lord God is upon me, / because the LORD has anointed me / to bring good tidings to the afflicted; / he has sent me to bind up the brokenhearted, / to proclaim liberty to the captives, / and the opening of the prison to those who are bound; / to proclaim the year of the LORD's favor" (Is 61:1–2).
- Jesus' healings were signs of messianic fulfillment, as we see in the conversation between Jesus and Martha just before he raises her brother Lazarus from the dead. "Jesus said to her, 'Your brother will rise again.' Martha said to him, 'I know that he will rise again in the resurrection at the last day.' Jesus said to her, 'I am the resurrection and the life; he who believes in me, though he die, yet shall he live, and whoever lives and believes in me shall never die. Do you believe this?' She said to him, 'Yes, Lord; I believe that you are the Christ, the Son of God, he who is coming into the world'" (Jn 11:23–27).
- The healings he performed showed Jesus' authority over sin and the troubles of the world, even illness and death. (The following chapters of this book will offer numerous examples of this.)
- Jesus' healings reveal his mercy, kindness, and compassion, as we see when he heals blind Bartimaeus (which we will explore in chapter 3), or when he tells the leper he does want him to be healed, saying, "I will; be clean" (which we will read about in chapter 5).

Again, in our limited human capacity, even with all that has been revealed by Christ and explained by saints and theologians, God's ways, as Isaiah 55:8–9 reminds us, will never be our ways; they will always be infinitely higher. The great contemporary theologian Dr. Peter Kreeft explains it beautifully:

> And Jesus' physical miracles of healing were literal, but they are also symbolic. For instance, when he heals the blind, that also symbolizes his spiritual healing of our inward eyes, our wisdom, the taking away of our foolishness, and eventually the beatific vision of the face of God in heaven. And when he makes the ears of the deaf to hear, that really literally happened, but it also symbolizes the fact that he makes the ears of our soul to hear God's will, which is God's beautiful music for our lives, God's providential plan for the story of our lives, in which God allows many evils and many kinds of evil to enter our lives but also delivers us from all of them in the end. The bottom line is that many passages in the Bible can be both literal and symbolic.

One of my favorite aspects of the Catholic Faith involves the witness of all the holy men and women who came before us, persevered in their quest to live out the call to heroic virtue, and became saints. Many years ago, my spiritual director suggested I find a saint with whom to spend some quality time, preferably a saint who had left behind writings I could meditate on, slowly, just a few minutes a day, and thus grow in my own personal holiness. I chose, or maybe she chose me, St. Teresa of Ávila because I connected with her spunk and tenacity in dealing with physical trials. After years of navigating many different ailments — some eventually rectified, others ongoing — reading of how Teresa dealt with her own maladies was encouraging and insightful. In her autobiography she writes:

> So strong were the medicines that after two months I was almost dead … I was in such agony that they feared I might go mad. … That night I had an attack which left me insensible for almost

> four days. They gave me the Sacrament of Extreme Unction, and in every minute of every hour thought that I was dying. They never stopped reciting the Creed to me, as though I could have heard what was said. At times they were so sure that I was dead that afterwards I actually found some wax on my eyelids. … For a day and a half, a grave was left open in my convent, waiting for my body; and the rites for the dead were performed at a friary of our Order a short distance away. … When I saw myself so paralyzed and still so young, and how the physicians of the world had dealt with me, I decided to invoke those of heaven to heal me. For though I bore my illness most joyfully, I still wanted to get well. But sometimes I reflected that I might regain my health and yet be lost, and that it would be better to stay as I was. But I always thought that I should serve God much better if I recovered. This is our mistake, never to resign ourselves absolutely to what the Lord does, though He knows best what suits us.

Every one of us should have a "saint posse" — a band of saints we can relate to, learn from, and turn to in times of trouble. Think about it. Which saint (or saints) could you invoke to journey with you as you read this book about seeking the assistance of the Divine Physician? My saint posse over the years has included Saint Faustina (to help me with my anxiety); Saint Gemma Galgani (for my daughter's scoliosis); Saint Peter (for my back pain); and Blessed Solanus Casey (to help me with my severe eczema). My group of saint friends is ever-growing and changing, but the Blessed Virgin Mary, Queen of All Saints, is always at the head of the pack. No one can nurse a child back to physical, emotional, or spiritual health like a mother, especially a mother who is "full of grace" as Mary is. As Venerable Patrick Peyton said, "If God chose her to be His mother, she must be someone special; God can't make a mistake. What's good enough for Him is good enough for me. I'm going to trust her, believe in her, and give myself to her protection."

Burdens Brought to Jesus

What brings you to Jesus? As we read further in this study, we'll discover the throngs of people who came to Jesus for healing and various types of assistance. I suppose you could sum it up that people came to listen to Jesus because they needed something. Maybe they didn't even consciously know what that something was, but somehow, they knew whatever it was, it would be found in Jesus. Some people came because they heard he could heal; the Gospels tell us that Jesus cured the sick. Was that enough to make them leave their homes and endure the discomfort of travel in the ancient world? Is that what they needed? Suffering, afraid, broken, probably having exhausted every avenue of healing they knew — when all they had tried failed — they sought this man. Stories of his healings, the miracles, the unexplained, but most importantly, hope drew them to come and see. No one like Jesus existed before, and two thousand years later, we know no one like him has or will come again. What had they heard? What did they expect? Is whatever attracted the earlier disciples to Jesus the same thing that brought you to enter into this study?

One of Jesus' most dramatic miracles wasn't a physical healing, but the feeding of a hungry crowd who had gathered to hear him teach. People came in droves: thousands of men, women, and children. They crowded the banks where he disembarked from his boat on the Sea of Galilee, finding places where they could see and, more importantly, hear this mysterious miracle man. Were they discontented in their circumstances, spiritually, economically, politically? Were they just curious? Perhaps some came to discover for themselves if this Jesus of Nazareth was truly from God. Was the arduous trek worth it? Was the desire to learn more of the hope, promise, and mercy offered through his testimonies enough to endure the hardship of travel? Would we have journeyed those miles to listen to this man?

Crowds came from their homes; whatever their motives were, they arrived. Moved by the multitudes, Jesus seized this opportunity to do what he did best: teach and heal. He cured their sickness and spent the day among them. Moved by pity and compassion, he tirelessly gave, no doubt touching many hearts, converting many souls, and stirring the desire of many to become disciples. On this day, in this location, they found an abundance of many things: grace, hope, mercy, tenderness, and love.

But they lacked food. He gave them sustenance of mind and spirit, but could this man provide for the body as well? Could he really be the answer to everything we need?

The day was coming to a close when the apostles approached the Master, imploring him to dismiss the crowds, knowing most would not leave of their own accord. In the presence of such greatness, witnessing things they'd never seen before, it would be difficult, maybe impossible, to get them to move from this place. How many times have we had mountaintop experiences — splendid, special days we never want to end? How many gathered around Jesus that day, like Peter at the Transfiguration, wished the day to go on forever? These wise men, his chosen apostles, knew only Jesus could move this group to disperse.

Jesus instead ordered the crowds to be seated and called for the meager amount of food the apostles were able to gather — five loaves of bread and two fish. With the people seated and at rest, Jesus lifted the burden of the day and their hunger by a simple command. In this short time with Jesus, they had learned to trust in him. They had come to yoke themselves to the teachings of this rabbi. "Come to me, all who labor, hunger, and thirst," Jesus urged them as he urges us, and he promises to take our burdens upon himself and give us rest. We see that promise in his ordering the vast crowd to be seated. Do you see Jesus' promises as trustworthy? Would you have sat and waited for him to act, or would you have doubted and gone to care for your own needs?

Taking the sparse offerings, Jesus presented them to the Father, blessed them, and broke them — dividing them among those who put their trust in him to provide. Not only was there enough to feed those present, but twelve bushels of fragments were left, collected, and no doubt distributed to others in need. When we seek what Jesus is offering, we are given rest. We are filled with more than we need and left with some to distribute to others who also need but have perhaps never even met Jesus, or do not yet realize what he is offering.

So I ask you again, what brings you to Jesus? What has led you to this Bible study about Jesus as our healer? I encourage you to pause here and pray about this for a few moments. Then, use the space provided to write down whatever is on your heart.

In this book, I've included many of the encounters from the Scriptures where Jesus heals. The accounts of healing are so numerous that I could not do them all justice in this short study. At its core, however, each encounter illustrates a foundation of faith. Moreover, each person who receives this incredible gift of a return to wholeness glorifies God through conversion and service, and by making the Good News known to others. Those who were healed by Jesus didn't keep the blessing of the moment to themselves but put it into some form of action. We are called to do the same. When Jesus touches our lives, it is not meant for us alone but is a call to each of us to go forth and make disciples of all nations.

How This Study Works

The chapters in this book can be read, reflected on, and studied individually or with a group of friends, or even with strangers who can become friends. Each chapter follows the same structure:

- **Opening Prayer:** Always begin with prayer, as that opens the communication with the Holy Spirit necessary to learn anything about the Faith. You can read the prayer that is written in this book, or you may choose to offer your own instead or in addition to that prayer.
- **Encounter with the Word:** The initial inspiration for the Stay Connected Journals came from a desire to provide a novel and engaging approach for women to grow in their faith through the Scriptures. While previous volumes in this series include an abundance of Bible verses, I desired to be even more intentional in how the word of God would guide the theme of each chapter. With that in mind, I have carefully chosen a special verse for each chapter as a place to pause, reflect, pray, and prepare.
- **On My Heart:** This section allows you to pause and contemplate the upcoming chapter for yourself. Use this journaling space to jot down what is currently occupying your thoughts, what you expect (or desire) to discover in the chapter, or what you may feel is a current need for healing.

- **Encounter with Christ:** In this section, we will reflect on the chapter's main topic, including the Scripture that inspired the chapter, along with personal witness and stories of encounter with Jesus.
- **An Invitation to Ponder:** This section is for you to go deeper with Jesus after reading and reflecting on encounters with Christ. You may choose to include your answers during group discussion if you wish, but this section is specifically meant to be a private moment, allowing you to share your thoughts with Jesus and to journal if you wish.
- **Connecting with Scripture:** Here, you will find Scriptures related to the overarching theme of the chapter. The space provided can be for writing out the entire verse or scribbling down some notes inspired by your reading. This journal is yours; I promise, no one will collect and correct your answers! You may also notice that, unlike some Bible studies, there are no "answers" in the back. Nor have I, in most cases, provided the text of the Scripture verses. I intentionally left them for you to look up because, early in my own study of Scripture, I quickly realized the Lord didn't always communicate with me through the verse the author instructed me to look up. With my nose in the actual Bible, the Holy Spirit would often wow me with inspirations and insights I never imagined! Finally, I recommend making these additional verses a central part of group discussions if you are using this study with others. While the Church provides interpretation of Scripture for teaching, it also allows freedom for personal reflection when reading the Bible; it is enthralling to discover all the ways the Lord speaks to us through his word!
- **An Invitation to Share:** This section includes questions to contemplate on your own or discuss with a group.
- **Closing Prayer:** Each chapter ends with prayer. Again, you may use the prayer written in this book, or you may choose to pray your own prayer. Prayer is a wonderful way to con-

clude your time with the Lord. Think of it as sending Jesus a thank you card for the gift of his time, love, and grace!

Most importantly, this book is designed to facilitate an easy, engaging, and (I hope) entertaining way to enter into the Scriptures — the living word of God. I love using the Internet to look up a quick Bible verse, and I have a Bible app on my phone, but nothing compares to holding my much loved, held-together-by-old-duct-tape, physical Bible. A physical Bible can be blessed, unlike your Kindle or smartphone, and it is a sacramental (an object of devotion that prepares one's soul for grace). I suggest keeping your Bible with you as you read this book, since I will recommend many Scripture passages for you to read and reflect on, and I will not always offer the actual text of those verses. Only the Holy Spirit knows which of his words will bring you the greatest comfort, insight, and enlightenment. Only he can illuminate the way for you to experience a deeper devotion. I can send you in the direction I was led, but only the Spirit can truly guide you to where you need to be. So get your Bible brushed off (or ordered) and prepare to delight yourself in the Lord, who longs to heal you and give you the desires of your heart.

ONE

Healed Past and Moving Forward

Opening Prayer

Come, Holy Spirit, open my heart and mind to receive the blessings and graces prepared specifically for me in this chapter on the many ways we can be healed when we open our hearts to encounter Jesus. Inspire within my soul a deep understanding of the truth that Jesus genuinely cares about me and my wellbeing. Help me to trust in his gentleness and deep, abiding love. Spirit of Truth, soften my heart as Jesus meets me exactly where I am in my life, regardless of my sins and broken places, to offer me redemption.

May I encounter Jesus with a curious hope, not dismissing his words or running away in fear or doubt. I long to receive the powerful, transforming message of his salvation and healing, as did the woman of Samaria. As I enter this time with the Lord through the Scriptures, reflection, and discussion, may I put aside all my worries, trepidation, uncertainty, and thoughts of being unworthy or, even worse, the lie that I am beyond help.

Give me the boldness to remain with the Messiah, attentively listening to the promises of abundant life and the renewal only he brings. Precious Spirit, please loosen anything binding my heart that prevents me from drinking deeply of the Living Water Jesus has come to give me. I long to know the many gifts of God. Come, Holy Spirit, so I may hear Jesus tell me all I ever did and be inspired to change, not despair. May this encounter transform my relationship with Christ so I may come to believe he is indeed the Savior of the world, just like the Samaritans who heard the testimony of the woman when she returned from the well.

Encounter with the Word

Many Samaritans from that city believed in him because of the woman's testimony, "He told me all that I ever did." So when the Samaritans came to him, they asked him to stay with them; and he stayed there two days. And many more believed because of his word. They said to the woman, "It is no longer because of your words that we believe, for we have heard for ourselves, and we know that this is indeed the Savior of the world." — John 4:39–42

On My Heart

Encounter with Christ

Jesus meets us where we are. We see this in a powerful way in the encounter described in the fourth chapter of the Gospel of John, where we read about Jesus' meeting with the Samaritan woman at the well. In the Eastern rites, the Samaritan woman in this story is known as Saint Photina. Here, we see a recurrent theme in the Gospel stories: Not only was Jesus there for those who encountered him, but he never left them the same way. There was always some form of healing in the encounter, and often a ripple effect from that healing reached others. That was the real story — that was what people needed to see.

Remarkably, as we learn from the Gospel accounts of his earthly ministry, in his every action and encounter, Jesus heals. Even when he doesn't physically make us well in the way we may hope, he can significantly transform us if we are open to it.

Reading the Samaritan woman's story of encountering Jesus at the well catapulted my faith to heights I never considered reaching for. Photina wasn't perfect, but Jesus loved her anyway. She had made many, many mistakes, and yet he came specifically to meet her where she was, in all her brokenness, shame, and sin. His love for her was unconditional. And just as Jesus did this for her, he also wants to do it for us.

The first striking detail of John 4 is subtle, easy to miss (and evidence that it is a good idea to read Scripture along with a good Catholic commentary). John 4:4 states that Jesus "had to pass through Samaria." This suggests he was in Sychar (Samaria) at that well, in that exact moment, not by coincidence, but very purposefully: to meet the Samaritan woman. Next, Saint John notes the hour of day when Jesus met Photina was noon. I don't know about you, but the last place I want to be at the height of the day's heat is in the desert sun. Yet there she was, gathering water away from the judgmental eyes of her neighbors, and Jesus waited to meet her where she was — physically, spiritually, mentally, and emotionally. He came to talk and gently guide her along a new path — to initiate a conversion.

Photina's brokenness in this Gospel story is both emotional and spiritual. It is clear she has some kind of faith, as she recognizes that someone is coming who will be their savior, the Messiah. Through her discussion with Jesus, she comes to know and believe that he is that someone. Some seeds of faith had already been planted in her heart so she would be able to recognize him. Yet she had been living far from the way God wants us to live. She had lived not in freedom, but as a slave to her sins. This encounter with Jesus transforms her life. He heals her emotional wounds — the scars of a life not lived well, whether by her own choices or because of circumstances beyond her control. We don't know the details of her five previous failed marriages and how she came to be living with man number six. The beauty is that those details didn't matter to Jesus! His mercy does not come with caveats.

Her response to this encounter with Jesus is to tell others. She leaves her old life behind, symbolized by leaving her water jar (v. 28), and goes home to evangelize. She can't keep the Good News to herself, and her technique is the best method of bringing people to Christ: personal witness. She simply shares what Jesus did for her. Many others also find healing thanks to her courage and unselfish act of boldly declaring Christ as Messiah to anyone who would listen. She no longer needs to hide in the midday sun! She is reintegrated into her community, where she publicly and openly shares her wounds and her remarkable transformation.

Her example proves we do not need to argue or attempt to convince anyone to follow Jesus. We simply need to tell our story and pray that others will seek out the same encounter with Jesus. In Photina's case, her neighbors left her and found Jesus for themselves, and they came to believe. Jesus healed Photina's spiritual brokenness and offered her new life in him. If he was willing to do this for her, he can also do so for us.

We see his willingness to heal us — even in our sinfulness — in another passage in John's Gospel (see 8:1–11), where we read of another woman — a woman brought in to test Jesus. She is being accused of adultery, a crime punishable by stoning. Many of the women I know don't need others to bring them before Christ to be tried. They are far too quick to point accusatory fingers at themselves. We are so tough on ourselves, believing we are defined by our past mistakes and not worthy of Jesus' mercy and forgiveness. Jesus does not condemn the woman caught in adultery; instead, he offers her freedom to live in his glorious light of redemption, telling her to go forth and sin no more. There is no sin he will not forgive. The only barrier lies in our free will and our refusal to accept his mercy.

Moreover, as we learn from the woman at the well, Jesus heals our past. He told Photina everything that she had done, not as a final, condemning act of judgment, but to allow her to feel better — to heal. It is not healthy to stifle or block memories, though we often think that is the best way to control, handle, and navigate through them.

In my own life, childhood trauma lay dormant in my memories for many years until my early twenties, when all those repressed memories came flooding back. That was a dark time. Through counseling, I began to emerge from self-loathing, shame, and guilt, most of which were not mine to be carrying. However, it wasn't until I was in my thirties, when I reverted back to my Catholic faith and embraced its devotion, that I truly started to feel Christ's healing in my life.

As I prayed, read the Scriptures, and participated in the sacraments, especially the Sacrament of Reconciliation, Jesus was able to heal me so completely that I even began to forget I had ever been that child who had endured so much. Now, it's typically not until somebody mentions a similar situation that I recall and think, *Oh yeah, that was me, too*. That's the power of grace, and that is what I wish for anyone reading this book: not only that you will seek God for physical healing and wellbeing, but more importantly, that you will seek God for spiritual and mental healing and wholeness that this world cannot give.

I want you to be able to look at yourself in the mirror and know you are fearfully and wonderfully made. God doesn't make junk, as my grandmother would say. You are worthy of his love and can be redeemed from anything you have done in the past, and healed of anything that has been done to you. Trust God fully and do not live in the past, because we cannot go back; we can only move forward — and forward is where God is.

While the ultimate goal of this life is not this life, but eternal life — immortality with God in heaven forever — we also have the reminder from the saints that, as Catherine of Siena taught, "all the way to heaven is heaven." What a grace to live in the hope of heaven while experiencing the joy of coming to know God more deeply and striving to live our lives more centered on him. At the same time, this life also involves suffering. As we read in Luke's Gospel, "And he said to all, 'If any man would come after me, let him deny himself and take up his cross daily and follow me. For whoever would save his life will lose it; and whoever loses his life for my sake, he will save it. For what does it profit a man if he gains the whole world and loses or forfeits himself?'" (9:23–25).

I know that it's difficult to wrap our minds around that. We are carnal beings who see only the world before us; believing in the invisible and the unknown is not easy. Yet God never asks us for the impossible. And he never promises something he doesn't intend to bring to fruition entirely. One of my favorite Scripture passages is in the Gospel of Matthew, where Jesus tells us, "Ask, and it will be given you; seek, and you will find; knock, and it will be opened to you. For every one who asks receives, and he who seeks finds, and to him who knocks it will be opened" (Mt 7:7–8). Have you ever considered asking God to reveal his presence to you in such a way that you would no longer have to live in fear or doubt, but could come to believe he is always with you, no matter what crosses he may ask you to carry?

God answered me in just the way I needed when I finally asked him for this grace. A few years ago, the Holy Spirit nudged me outside to pray. At first, I assumed it was to keep me away from the distractions of my desk, home, and phone, but it turned out he had bigger plans. Since I live on a busy street, I decided to do laps around the perimeter of my yard as I prayed. As I made my last circuit, wrestling with all the knots of my life, I looked to heaven and aired my grievances. "Lord," I prayed, "what is it you want from me? I never miss Sunday Mass, and I diligently pray the Rosary. I have even given my life to telling people how awesome you are, and this is my reward? A life overflowing with many hardships — illness, death, financial difficulties, and family discord! Again, Lord, I ask, what do you want from me?"

As I completed the behind-the-house leg of my Rosary walk and turned, now facing the highway that runs along the front of my home, a tractor-trailer passing by caught my attention. On the side of the truck, in giant red letters, was the word *FIDELITY*. Faithfulness. How could I ignore the timing of the truck's appearance? This had to be an answer to my cry of distress. Only God could arrange the precision of that moment. Furthermore, I had spent twenty years watching traffic along that same highway, and this was the first time I had ever seen that truck.

My trust grew exponentially from that "Godcidence" moment on. While the world may see this situation as a coincidence, I knew it to be heaven reaching through the veil to assure me everything is possible with faith. Fidelity: Just be faithful. I can certainly work on that, continuing to pray, hope, wait, and trust — one rosary bead at a time. Since I first saw that Fidelity truck during my Rosary, the Lord has sent them again and again. Recently, as I drove and prayed, I realized it had been a while since I had seen one. I thought maybe the company had gone out of business. On this particular morning, driving to work and praying the Rosary, I began the Apostles' Creed, "I believe in God ..." and I got completely sidetracked. I wondered, *Do I really believe in God? I mean there's so much that I don't know about God; I cannot see him, and I only hear him through his word and through the voice of the priest, and often in my own head.* For a moment, I thought I needed a Fidelity truck to get myself back on track. But then I stopped myself. I prayed instead, "Lord, I want to believe in you because of who you are and not because of the signs and wonders you send me."

Yet the Lord knows my heart, and he had great pity on me. That very moment, I saw a Fidelity truck in the road in front of me. I laughed and cried as the Lord often makes me do when he surprises me with grace. If you, like me, need that sign and wonder to have your heart reassured, I ask you to trust the Lord and ask him to show you, in whatever way he wishes. Jesus never abandons or forsakes us, as he's promised in the Scriptures, and he will be with us always; he is real and very, very faithful.

Encounters with Jesus transform us, just as they transformed the life of the woman at the well. Just as he did for her, Jesus wants to meet us where we are and heal our emotional wounds. He can even heal the scars of a life not well lived. We don't know if Photina's situation was the result of her own choices or circumstances beyond her control, or both. The beauty is that it didn't matter to Jesus! His mercy doesn't come with caveats. Photina's response to encountering the Messiah was to go tell others — to evangelize. She couldn't keep it to herself, and her technique was a personal witness: sharing what Jesus did for her. How many others discovered healing in their lives because of her courage and selflessness in fully proclaiming Christ?

An Invitation to Ponder

Where is your well? Jesus meets us where we are right now, regardless of our spiritual, emotional, or physical state. He longs for a meaningful encounter with us. Jesus met Saint Photina at the well, where she went daily to draw water. Take a few moments to imagine Jesus meeting you in an ordinary moment in your life, as it is right now. Where would Jesus meet you in your daily life? Where (or how) might Jesus find you? Do you believe he wants to meet you there? Do you fear your past will exclude you from a relationship with Jesus?

When I begin to lose hope that I will meet Jesus at my well, I remember this awe-inspiring psalm: "What is man that you are mindful of him, / and the son of man that you care for him? / Yet you have made him little less than the angels, / and you have crowned him with glory and honor" (Ps 8:4–5). Jesus wants to meet you exactly where you are.

Use the journaling space below to record your answers to the questions above and whatever else this reflection has stirred in your heart.

Connecting with Scripture

I find it remarkable how the themes in the Bible intertwine, creating a rich tapestry from the interwoven threads of the Old and New Testaments. Learning to encounter the Triune God — Father, Son, and Holy Spirit — throughout the verses is life-changing and spiritually transformative. In this section, I have added five verses to draw us deeper into this chapter's theme of the many ways we can be healed when we open our hearts to encounter Jesus. Use the space provided to jot down notes and words or even transcribe the entire verse — whatever best helps you reflect and pray.

Pray: Come, Holy Spirit, guide me as I read and reflect on these Scripture verses and any others you may reveal to me during this time with my Bible. Shower me with all the wisdom, knowledge, and understanding I need to allow your word to dwell in me richly. Amen.

Psalm 130

Job 38

Luke 13:10–17

Luke 14:1–6

Romans 5:8

As the psalmist sings, "Hope in the LORD! / For with the LORD there is mercy, / and with him is plenteous redemption" (Ps 130:7). I love the word *plenteous*. What a poetic way of saying *plentiful*, *copious*, *abundant*, and even *lavish* amounts of something! The Lord does not hold back anything from his beloved, especially the gifts only he can give, such as mercy, grace, faith, peace, and joy. This plenteous redemption has no limits; it reaches far into our past, deep into our today, and well into our future.

Few people suffer to the extent of poor Job in the Old Testament. By no cause of his own, Job endured the loss of children, livestock, livelihood, material possessions, and his own health. His wife proved to be little comfort (but let's face it, the woman was also going through some serious trauma, so I think we should give her a pass on this one). Job's friends were wonderful (see Jb 2:11–13) until they weren't (4—37). They demonstrated how to comfort a friend in need by coming to be with him, sitting in silence, and being present simply so he would not be alone. Then they started talking and, in my humble opinion, ruined all the good they had previously accomplished by coming to the aid of their friend. Sometimes, in our desire to affirm, validate, or even comfort others, we get into trouble, because most of us have no idea of God's plan for others' suffering.

The *Ignatius Catholic Study Bible* describes the importance of the dialogue between Job and his friends this way:

> Following more than thirty chapters of intense dialogue, the debate between Job and his friends ends in a stalemate. Neither Job nor they have surrendered an inch to the other. However, in the final chapters of the book, God comes to Job in the winds of a tempest and lectures him about the limitless power and wisdom of the Almighty (chaps. 38–41). … [Job] has learned that divine Providence is alive and well in the world, even in the lives of individuals. More than that, he has come to see that true wisdom is found in humility before God; after all, some things are simply beyond human comprehension. This insight is directly relevant to his situation: although Job is never informed of the reason why he was made to suffer, he has

> come to trust that God is just and that he knows what is best for him. If the Lord is in sovereign control of all things, then, rest assured, suffering is not meaningless, even if it remains a mystery. At times, it may be a form of divine discipline for our faults (5:17–18), but suffering can also increase our virtue, our merits, and our reliance upon God. The latter is true of Job, who is tested and found faithful. To make this clear to all, the Lord doubles his blessings to Job and restores his health and happiness once more (42:10–17).

Sometimes, we have to wait on the Lord. However, I find it comforting that Job was not left destitute. That is true of two seemingly random encounters with Jesus in the Gospel of Luke, both of which affirm his willingness to meet (and heal) us wherever we are.

First, we read of the woman crippled for eighteen years (see Lk 13:10–17). Next, the physician, Luke, introduces us to the man with dropsy (edema or swelling) in his hand (14:1–6). Like the encounter with Saint Photina, both of these encounters appear to be random; however, Jesus is God. He knew where each of these people would be and that they were in need of healing. There are no coincidences where God is concerned. I know people have many different terms for divine intervention, but my favorite is *Godcidence*. When reading the word of God, it is fascinating to pay attention to subtleties, such as the fact that Jesus was dining at a Pharisee's home in Luke 14. Jesus is so willing to meet us at *any* place, and he wants to heal everyone. It was not only the crippled woman or the man with dropsy the Lord came to transform with these encounters. He wants those who witness these miracles to experience a conversion of heart and healing of their own. And he does not wait for us to become perfect, as Saint Paul reminds us in Romans 5:6–8; rather, he takes us exactly as we are, broken places and all.

An Invitation to Share

The Samaritan woman evangelized by simply sharing her encounter with Jesus. If you are reading this study, I suspect you've had some experience of faith that draws you to continue to follow Jesus. What was that experience?

How did it change you? Is there someone in your life with whom you could share it to help pique their curiosity about Jesus — and if yes, who is that person?

Is there a past hurt or circumstance that may be holding you back from seeking or receiving healing? What is it? If you are unsure, sit with this question in prayer, asking the Holy Spirit to reveal any wounds or resentments that are keeping you from being open to his work in your life.

The crippled woman in Luke's Gospel waited eighteen years to be healed. We don't know much about her, but her presence in the synagogue reveals she was a woman of some faith. In the Old Testament, Job watched his life go from bad to worse without knowing if things would ever change, yet he never lost faith. What are some of the ways you keep your faith as you wait on the Lord?

Closing Prayer

O, Spirit of Truth, the Paraclete, continue the good work you have begun in me. Open my heart and mind to receive the healing encounters and release from past hurts you have prepared specifically for me. Please help me to discover the beauty of your merciful, tender love. Show me where Jesus desires to meet me, exactly where I am, regardless of my sins and broken places, and bring me healing.

May I encounter Jesus with openness. Precious Spirit, help me not to dismiss the spiritual nudges in my heart or run in fear as I feel myself drawing closer to Jesus. I long to receive the powerful, transforming message of redemption, salvation, and healing, as did Saint Photina. Show me how to put aside all fear, trepidation, and uncertainty. Remove from my mind all thoughts of being unworthy or beyond help. God alone offers abundant life and the renewal of hope. Prepare my heart to receive and cooperate with all your gifts and fruits.

Come, Holy Spirit, to loosen anything binding my heart that prevents me from drinking deeply of the Living Water Jesus has come to offer me. Let my eyes be open to recognize unexpected encounters with Jesus, so he may tell me all I ever did and inspire me to change and not to despair. May this encounter help me believe that Jesus is indeed my Lord and my Savior and make me willing to share that testimony with others.

TWO

Do You Want to Be Well?

Opening Prayer

Come, Holy Spirit, open my heart and mind to receive the blessings and graces prepared specifically for me in this chapter on recognizing when I am paralyzed by circumstances, succumbing to my perceived limitations and fears. Inspire within me a clearer understanding of the truth that Jesus genuinely cares about my life and wellbeing, as well as those of whom I love. Help me to trust in his faithfulness, unafraid to approach him with all that weighs upon my heart and burdens my soul.

May I encounter Jesus with a curious hope, not dismissing his words or running away in fear or doubt. I long to receive the powerful, transforming message of his salvation and healing, as did the man who laid beside the pool, waiting for thirty-eight years to be healed. As I enter this time with the Lord through the Scriptures, reflection, and discussion, may I put aside all my worries that I am beyond help or that no one will come to my assistance when I ask.

Mighty Consoler, please give me the courage to step into

the stirred-up water of renewal only Jesus can truly bring. Generous Spirit, please loosen anything binding my heart that prevents me from accepting Jesus' loving attention. I long to know the many gifts of God. Come, Holy Spirit, so I may accept Jesus' offer of healing. I want to be healed by my Lord and my Savior. Grant me greater trust in his power and desire to heal me.

Encounter with the Word

Now there is in Jerusalem by the Sheep Gate a pool, in Hebrew called Beth-za'tha, which has five porticoes. In these lay a multitude of invalids, blind, lame, paralyzed. One man was there, who had been ill for thirty-eight years. When Jesus saw him and knew that he had been lying there a long time, he said to him, "Do you want to be healed?" The sick man answered him, "Sir, I have no man to put me into the pool when the water is troubled, and while I am going another steps down before me." —J ohn 5:2–7

On My Heart

Encounter with Christ

Do you want to be healed? Do you ever feel like you are just waiting for someone to lift you into God's healing waters? What if, once cleansed of your ailment, you could return again and again for further assurance of healing — a spiritual refresher? In John's Gospel (5:1–16), we read about a man who has been crippled for over thirty eight years. He has long desired to experience the healing power of God. This Gospel challenges us to consider not only the remarkable healing power of Christ, but also his compassion and mercy.

After reflecting on this conversation between the man and Jesus, it occurred to me that I am highly dependent on others in all areas of my life. We all are! There are aspects of my finances that are dependent on my employer, of my health that are reliant on my doctor, and of my spiritual wellbeing that are conditioned on my priest. Ultimately, however, the most important dependency I will ever have is on Jesus. Yet my faith in

Jesus does not negate my need for other people; each is an integral part of attaining that wellbeing I desire. I need other people in my life (like my employer, my doctor, and faithful priests) to figuratively lift me into the "healing waters" of financial responsibility, good health, and faithfulness. Yet when I rely most of all on Jesus, as John's Gospel illustrates, so much more is possible — even miracles.

"Jesus said to him, 'Rise, take up your pallet, and walk.' And at once the man was healed, and he took up his pallet and walked" (Jn 5:8–9).

Before healing him, Jesus asked the man if he wanted to be healed. Did the man truly want to be well? Some people seem happy being unhappy. They may seem like they are working on a change in their health, work situation, or home life, but they never appear to make any strides forward. Each time you speak with them, it is the same story, as if they've just put their life on auto-repeat. Is it fear of the unknown? It's easy to get comfortable with what we know, even if it makes us miserable. I struggled for years to make changes to my diet, even though gluten and dairy were making me violently ill, because I hated missing out on what everyone else was enjoying. Oh, birthday parties were so hard! Fear of missing out is very real. Maybe the man at the pool, in some strange way, found comfort in the life he knew and never sought help so as not to have to make any real change. Perhaps he feared that the hope that sustained him — the hope that one day he'd make it into the pool as the water swirled — would be dashed if it did not work. And then what? "Then what?" Those two little words have so much power!

At first, this passage in John's Gospel appears to be all about the physical healing that takes place. However, as always happens when we encounter Christ, there is more. In this story, we see Jesus' concern for our spiritual wellbeing. Tucked into this Scripture are two little nuggets I wish to unpack with you. I will work backward here, so bear with me. At the end of Jesus' encounter with the man, John includes this exchange, "Afterward, Jesus found him in the temple, and said to him, 'See, you are well! Sin no more, that nothing worse befall you'" (Jn 5:14). When I first read Jesus' words, I took it as a stern warning; however, the more I sat with the verse and prayed for the Spirit's enlightening, something in my heart shifted. Recognizing Jesus' inherent tenderness and genuine concern for those entrusted to him by the Father, the salutation felt more like cautionary advice from a caring friend. See, I have this theory about how the Lord works, and I've seen it play out in my life, again and again. The Lord allows something to happen in our life that is traumatic but not devastating because he wants us to be mindful of that moment and see the warning he has allowed, which helps us avoid something far worse in the future (especially something that involves sinful behavior).

In another Gospel passage, we witness a similar encounter. Jesus heals a crippled man, directly correlating the forgiveness of sins with the physical healing. A paralyzed man is lowered by his friends through the roof to be healed. As he did with the man lying at the pool, Jesus instructs the paralyzed man, "Take up your pallet." To the man at the pool, he continues, "and walk" (Jn 5:8), while he instructs the man lowered through the roof, "and go home" (Mk 2:11). In both encounters, Jesus makes it abundantly clear that the most important healing that has taken place is spiritual. He has the authority to forgive sins, which is even more powerful than restoring the physical movement of one's legs.

As theologian Dr. Peter Kreeft writes:

> It's harder for God to forgive sins than to heal cripples, because sinners resist but cripples don't. It cost God the life of his Son to forgive us our sins, but it cost him nothing to heal the cripple. That's the deeper point, and Jesus' audience didn't get it. But they got the obvious point, that it's easier to claim to forgive sins, which only God can do, than to claim to miraculously heal cripples, which also only God can do, because there's no proof that the sins are forgiven but there's physical proof that the cripple is healed. So Jesus did the harder thing to prove — the miracle — to show that he had the power to do what was really the harder thing to do — to buy our forgiveness at the price of his own body and blood.

The passage from John's Gospel describing the healing of the sick man at the pool includes a fascinating play on words. The sick man says he has no "man" to lift him into the water, yet Jesus will be the man to help. And his help, of course, will go far beyond putting someone in the water. He himself is the Living Water. Like the man lying by the pool, we similarly open ourselves to the movement of the Spirit in our lives when we welcome Jesus' assistance, thereby consenting and allowing him to enter into our paralyzing moments and lift us to a place where we can begin to heal. The healing we experience likely won't be a miracle as profound to the naked eye as a sick man being healed after thirty-eight years of illness, but this healing Jesus gives — when we allow it — will be no less profound.

There are so many ways we can be sick — physically, emotionally, mentally, spiritually; we even use the word *sick* to refer to being fed up with something. Most people do not wish to or like to be sick. As a mother, I have said on more than one occasion, "I don't have time to be sick." As a person with mysophobia (a form of OCD — an irrational fear of contamination), I probably take my dislike for being out of commission with any type of illness to a whole new level. The irony is, for a very long period of my life, I would have welcomed illness because it gave me a valid excuse to give in to my insecurities and fears. I would have happily taken a day or two on the couch with my tissues, soup, and favorite book instead of facing the world. Being sick was sometimes convenient and sometimes comforting because nothing was expected of me in that condition.

It would seem evident that the man in this Gospel did not wish to remain unwell, since he was lying so close to this place that promised him healing. Yet he does seem to have a few excuses to explain why he hasn't taken advantage of this cure for the last thirty-eight years. As I contemplated why he had not simply asked another person to help him or devised a way to get in a better position to receive the healing, I thought of that fearful time in my life — that time when change seemed almost as overwhelming and scary as remaining in my current condition. I remembered how my pride prevented me from reaching out to anyone for help, because I didn't want to blow my "I have it all together" image.

How hard it can be to enlist another person's assistance, especially when it means admitting — out loud — that you cannot help yourself. How frightening this step can be, especially when you wonder if you'll be turned down or disappointed after you have mustered the strength to ask. Likewise, how hard it is to humble myself before the Lord, admitting my sinfulness and need for a savior!

When I finally reached that point, I knew it was time to be well. The first person I turned to was Jesus. I returned to the Sacraments of Reconciliation and Eucharist (both in the liturgy and in adoration). I felt him ask me this same question: "Do you want to be well?" Answering "yes" came with the recognition that the healing was coming from Jesus (in whatever form he chose to send it), and this finally made it possible for me to accept it.

As I mentioned above, Jesus heals us, but he also warns us to avoid sin "that nothing worse befall you" (Jn 5:14). In my life, my first warning-blessing came many years ago when I prepared one of my first public presentations. I convinced a local parish to allow me to give a brief presentation about social media and evangelization. I was up almost all night preparing my PowerPoint presentation (not because I was diligent, but because I had procrastinated until the very last moment). The next morning, I awoke with a start, checked my watch, and realized I had slept through the entire thing! I called the good deacon who had graciously invited me to speak. Absolutely humiliated, and through tears, I profusely apologized. On the other end of the receiver, I heard laughter! What an odd response to the position I had just put this man in. He chuckled again and said, "The Lord must really love you, because not a single person arrived for your presentation." From that moment on, not only did I prepare well ahead of time for my talks, but I also got to bed at a reasonable hour, set multiple alarms, and even left the window curtain open so the sun would wake me in the morning. I felt the Lord granted me a special grace in this embarrassing situation, encouraging me to make changes before my actions led to something far more devastating.

Another more comical example occurred more recently, during a very hectic time in my life, when I found myself focused on my vast to-do list and not on my surroundings. I was working remotely and had an early morning meeting, which meant I needed to move our family's two parakeets out of my home office. I grabbed the cage and headed for another room in the house that is decently out of earshot so I could have my meeting. Moments later, the birds and I were sprawled across our hallway floor, as I had tripped over a cord I hadn't seen. Bruised and battered, but luckily without dead birds, I saw this as a major wake-up call to be more vigilant and to pay attention, that nothing worse might befall me (or my family's pets).

I share these stories because I think it's important for us to remember that the misfortunes and irritations that befall us can be gifts. Remember, God can only do and will good, but due to the effects of original sin, our fallen nature, and free will, he does allow trials and tribulations in our lives. Yet when we open our hearts to his work in us and ask him to show us at that moment what the true lesson is, we may find that he allows difficulties to save us from much worse experiences. I can tell you, my birds are thrilled that I now know to hold them very carefully and watch every step I take when I'm carrying them anywhere. I've also seen the Lord do this in my health, relationships, and finances. When we allow ourselves to see the world through the eyes of God, every moment is an opportunity to learn and to grow, to put away our sinful past and to embrace the life God has for us. Jesus is indeed offering to make us well, especially by extending his mercy and forgiveness. He longs to see us whole, leaning on him with all our mind, heart, and soul, yet he respects our freedom and waits for us to be open to his work in our lives.

An Invitation to Ponder

Do you, like me, guard your "I have it all together" persona? Do you avoid asking for assistance out of fear your pleas for help will be rejected? What about coming to Jesus? Is it easier not to ask and find ways to manage or cope, because asking and not receiving may be just too much to bear? Ask yourself truthfully: Do you want to be well?

Use the journaling space below to record your answers to these questions and whatever else this reflection has stirred in your heart.

Connecting with Scripture

In this section, I have added five verses for you to reflect more deeply on this chapter's theme of recognizing when we are paralyzed by circumstances, giving in to limitations or fears that keep us from allowing the Lord to heal us as he desires. Use the space provided to jot down notes and words or even transcribe the entire verse — whatever fosters your prayer and reflection.

Pray: Come, Holy Spirit, guide me as I read and reflect on these Scripture verses and any others you may reveal to me during this time with my Bible. Shower me with all the wisdom, knowledge, and understanding I need to allow your word to dwell in me richly. Amen.

Psalm 103:2–4

Isaiah 53:3–6

John 1:14–18

2 Corinthians 1:3–7

2 Corinthians 4:16–18

As we reflect on Jesus' healing throughout this book, I would be remiss not to acknowledge that there are times when the Lord does not heal or answer our prayers exactly as we've asked. Rather, through wisdom beyond our comprehension, he allows the infirmity or affliction to continue because a greater good will come from the journey than would be produced by a miraculous cure.

Every living person, at one time or another in their lives, can expect to be afflicted in some way. Physically, mentally, emotionally, and yes, even spiritually, we struggle with our weak human condition. And if you like control, as I do, this can be extremely frustrating, even frightening. Because of our human condition, we are likely to face pain, suffering, and sadness. Thankfully, many diseases and illnesses can be rectified through the grace of modern medicine, and often these are gratefully quick fixes. Other conditions take longer to heal and require interventions like some form of therapy — mental or physical — and still others may never be healed this side of heaven. So, how do we navigate these swelling or terrifying waves when Jesus doesn't immediately calm the stormy seas?

In Isaiah 53, one of the passages about the Lord's Suffering Servant, the prophet foretells Jesus' suffering, which in turn reveals why Jesus understands our human afflictions so deeply. As we read in Hebrews 4:15, "For we have not a high priest who is unable to sympathize with our weaknesses." Jesus came to endure suffering for our benefit, bearing our grief, sorrows, and ultimately, our sins. Toward the end of the passage, Isaiah shifts the language, illustrating the temporal and eternal blessings, fruits, and satisfactions that afflictions offered for the benefit of others can bring. This conclusion, especially for those in the thick of a new diagnosis, or navigating chronic or uncurable conditions, requires a movement of faith that can only be embraced through an outpouring of grace from God.

Much of my faith lives in my head, and what should be a short journey to my heart is not unlike the Israelites wandering in the desert for forty years. The journey from Egypt to the Holy Land, had the Israelites not continued to fall into doubt and sin, would have been pretty direct. But because they did not trust, they had to remain in the desert for a long time. In a similar way, my own doubts, fears, and concupiscence often block me from simply accepting God's word and promises. In other words, my head knowledge fails to become heartfelt. That's typically when the Lord will send me a real-life experience to illustrate his point and help me find a shortcut on the journey, as he did for me on a retreat several years ago.

As we sat in the circle, waiting to be assigned our small-group room partner for our retreat weekend, I looked across the room at the young man in the wheelchair and embarrassingly thought to myself, "Anyone but him, Lord." It wasn't that I didn't love Val Monteiro, I was just very uncomfortable with the idea of what would be expected of me as his partner. He was almost completely paralyzed at that time from his advancing muscular dystrophy, and I knew there would be extra duties that I felt very unqualified to accomplish.

In Jesus' typical "this will be best for you" mode of operation, I was indeed paired up with Val. And as the Lord promised, his grace was sufficient, enabling me to undertake any care Val required over the weekend. Notably, I gained an incredible friend, found a new level of belly laugh I never knew existed within me (Val was a jokester), and developed a new appreciation for two stories in the Bible — one the healing of the paralytic, and the other, the healing of the man born blind. Val always wanted his illness to glorify God. I promised him that one day, if the Lord opened the door, I would make sure people learned of his incredible story. Here is part of it in Val's own words:

> I experienced the paschal mystery in my own life through Becker muscular dystrophy (BMD), a slower progressive form of the genetic disease that I was diagnosed with at five years old. My family

and friends have always treated me like anybody else. While growing up, I never thought that I had a disability because I did almost everything that everyone else did. I realized that I had a disability when I was twelve years old. I had surgery on my legs to loosen the muscles, and I had to learn how to walk all over again with difficulty. The first time after the surgery that I stood up on my legs, I could feel the incisions stretch and burn, but I fought through the pain and started walking again.

In the fall of 1993, as I began college along with the use of a wheelchair, I started to turn away from God. I used to cry myself to sleep, wondering why this was happening to me. I asked God, in anger, "What did I do to deserve this? Why me? Are you punishing me for something that I've done?" I didn't see any point in living a life like this. My world was crumbling all around me, and I felt miserable.

At that time, I didn't see any point in going to Mass, and I went just to keep my parents happy. During Mass, I heard the reading of the Gospel of John 9:1–3. "As he passed by, he saw a man blind from his birth. And his disciples asked him, 'Rabbi, who sinned, this man or his parents, that he was born blind?' Jesus answered, 'It was not that this man sinned, or his parents, but that the works of God might be made manifest in him.'"

After hearing that reading, I suddenly realized that it was ridiculous how I thought God was punishing me. I knew that God didn't put me in this wheelchair as a punishment. I realized that, in a weird way, this is actually a gift from God. I thought that if God can work through a blind man, why couldn't he work through me and my disability? My mission is to go out and show others what God's power, love, and mercy can do for us.

I used to ask to be healed, but after that miraculous day in Mass, I surrendered my life to God's loving hands. I realized God had blessed me with spiritual healing because I have accepted and experienced how God has worked through me and my disability to show others his great love. Even if I never receive a cure, that's all right with me. When the day comes that I die, that's when I'm

> going to be healed because I'm not taking the wheelchair with me.
>
> I've learned that we should give our sufferings up to Christ on the cross. We share in Christ's suffering on the cross whenever we suffer physical and emotional pain. Like Christ's suffering, our sufferings have a redemptive dimension for our salvation. Our challenges and difficulties can be given up for the sake of others, for their souls. I have consecrated my disability to the greater glory of God by giving up my struggles with BMD for the souls in purgatory, for my family and friends, and for those in most need. Suffering for others is the greatest sacrifice that we can make, and we imitate Christ and his sacrifice.

In a strange twist of God's mysterious designs, it was not the BMD that took Val's life but melanoma. In the many years I was blessed to be his friend, I watched him battle countless lung infections and near-death complications from his disease. He never lost his faith, sense of humor, or determination to use his story to always glorify God. Jesus may not have removed the burden of BMD from Val, but he gave him something much more valuable: an unshakable, unwavering faith in the goodness of God. Many people stepped into the light of Christ because of Val's witness as a good and faithful servant, and although I will never stop praying for the repose of his soul (it is dangerous to canonize a person before the Church has done so), there is a part of me that delights in the hope that he shares (or will soon share) in the Master's joy (see Mt 25:21).

The Catholic Church also has a powerful teaching on redemptive suffering — not an easy theology to share in the midst of a storm, but one every Christian should understand because, since we are human, we know there will be storms. In his apostolic letter *Salvifici Doloris* ("On Redemptive Suffering"), Pope St. John Paul II speaks of the sharers of the cross:

> Saint Paul speaks of various sufferings and, in particular, of those in which the first Christians became sharers "for the sake of Christ." These sufferings enable the recipients of that Letter to share in the work of the Redemption, accomplished through the suffering and death of the Redeemer. The eloquence of the

> Cross and death is, however, completed by the eloquence of the Resurrection. Man finds in the Resurrection a completely new light, which helps him to go forward through the thick darkness of humiliations, doubts, hopelessness and persecution. Therefore the Apostle will also write in the Second Letter to the Corinthians: "For as we share abundantly in Christ's sufferings, so through Christ we share abundantly in comfort too." Elsewhere he addresses to his recipients words of encouragement: "May the Lord direct your hearts to the love of God and to the steadfastness of Christ." And in the Letter to the Romans he writes: "I appeal to you therefore, brethren, by the mercies of God, to present your bodies as a living sacrifice, holy and acceptable to God, which is your spiritual worship."
>
> The very participation in Christ's suffering finds, in these apostolic expressions, as it were a twofold dimension. If one becomes a sharer in the sufferings of Christ, this happens because Christ has opened his suffering to man, because he himself in his redemptive suffering has become, in a certain sense, a sharer in all human sufferings. Man, discovering through faith the redemptive suffering of Christ, also discovers in it his own sufferings; he rediscovers them, through faith, enriched with a new content and new meaning. (*Salvifici Doloris,* 20)

One inspiring example of someone who embraced her cross with steadfast faithfulness was my very sweet friend Mary Joyce Phillips. A quadriplegic and in a wheelchair the majority of her life, she contracted polio at age seven and spent seven years in a hospital valiantly fighting the disease, including a significant amount of time in an iron lung. Mary Joyce once shared that she was one of the last people to become sick from polio during a 1955 epidemic, just months before the polio vaccine would be released. Confined to a wheelchair, unable to care for herself her entire life, her faith in the goodness of God never wavered. Mary Joyce credited her strong faith to the many years she spent in hospitals in the loving care of religious sisters. She would tell me they not only provided the necessary medical care for her body but, more importantly, they tended to the wellbeing of her soul. Intent on never wasting her suffering, she offered it up to the Lord in reparation for the sins of the world, especially for an end to abortion and for the conversion of souls, particularly those in her family.

Mary Joyce had a special devotion to Our Blessed Mother, always preferring to have her chair positioned in front of our parish's authentic replica of the image of Our Lady of Guadalupe, especially at the Masses she served as lector. I was awed during Mass to see her position her chair to mimic our postures. She would lean back to look at the Lord during the Consecration and tilt the chair forward when we were all bowing. Additionally, this remarkable woman spent hours in Eucharistic adoration. The Blessed Mother (I'm convinced) even worked out the details of her life to allow her to live in an assisted living facility right across the street from an adoration chapel! Her example of joy amid suffering and loving the Lord despite her difficult circumstances inspired all who were blessed to witness her faith in action.

Mary Joyce succumbed to COVID-19 just a month before effective treatments for the illness became available. This holy woman made me promise to pray for her after her death and never assume she was in heaven. To that end, I have Masses said for the repose of her soul and include her in my Divine Mercy Chaplet intentions. However, a part of me just can't help but imagine Mary Joyce and Val, free of their wheelchairs, dancing joyfully as they savor their eternal reward. As Val would say, "I am pretty sure there are no wheelchairs in heaven."

An Invitation to Share

What would be your answer to Jesus' question, "Do you want to be well?"

Do you fear change or, on the other hand, the very real possibility that a situation that is causing you suffering may not change, at least not as quickly as you wish? Think of a current area in your life where either of these fears may be keeping you from seeking the Lord's help. Can you place those fears before him and give him permission to act as he sees fit?

Saint Paul's message to the Corinthians that no suffering is wasted is a powerful one. Often the Lord allows us to connect with someone going through a suffering similar to something we have endured. If we allow it, the Lord can use us to speak comfort or hope into that person's situation, just as he did in ours. Consider some of the difficulties you have traversed in your life. Is there a way of paying forward the wisdom your scars have earned?

Closing Prayer

Mighty Consoler, continue the good work begun in me through the gifts of faith and grace. Open my heart and mind to receive the assistance prepared specifically for me as I continue through this book. Please help me to discover the beauty of Jesus' merciful, tender love offered through the kind words or actions of others. Please show me where Jesus wants to heal me and give me the courage to ask, even if I don't get the answers I seek (at least, not immediately). Bring consolation in the midst of suffering, bestowing upon me all the graces needed to traverse the road I find myself upon.

May I encounter Jesus with openness. Help me not to dismiss the word of God or run in fear from its teaching. I long to receive the powerful, transforming message of trusting in God's ways and perfect timing, as displayed by the healing of the man by the pool. Show me how to put aside all anxiety, distrust, and uncertainty of the future. Remove from my mind all thoughts of being unworthy or beyond help. Jesus alone offers abundant life and the renewal of hope. Open my heart to receive the gift of friendship and companions on the journey, especially those living with an affliction who offer others a way to grow in holiness.

Holy Spirit, please loosen anything binding my heart that prevents me from receiving Jesus' healing. Help me to know the many gifts of God. Come, Holy Spirit, so I may receive the Living Water himself, and give me the strength to hold onto hope through the toughest days. And may I share with others who are suffering the comfort I receive through this encounter with Jesus.

THREE

An Impaired Sense of Self and God

Opening Prayer

Come, Holy Spirit, open my heart and mind to receive the blessings and graces prepared specifically for me in this chapter on having the faith to cry out to Jesus, trusting that he is ever present, although we cannot see him. In my darkest moments, may I never forget the Lord is my remedy for all that befalls me. Spirit, rouse the strength within me to call boldly to him, and to be attentive to his response to that call.

Spirit of the Lord, may I never tire of coming in humble prayer to ask, seek, and knock, as Jesus instructed, believing my prayers will always be answered according to God's holy, loving, and perfect will. Strengthen my resolve never to grow weary in my circumstances, ever mindful that the answers I receive, although they may not be what I desire in my life or for those I love, always supply grace.

I long to know your many gifts, sweet Spirit of God —

faith, grace, joy, and eternal life, to name only a few. Come, Holy Spirit, so I may grow in grace and wisdom, trusting in your infinite wisdom over my weak, selfish desires. May this encounter further transform my relationship with Christ.

Encounter with the Word

And when he heard that it was Jesus of Nazareth, he began to cry out and say, "Jesus, Son of David, have mercy on me!" And many rebuked him, telling him to be silent; but he cried out all the more, "Son of David, have mercy on me!" And Jesus stopped and said, "Call him." And they called the blind man, saying to him, "Take heart; rise, he is calling you." And throwing off his cloak he sprang up and came to Jesus. And Jesus said to him, "What do you want me to do for you?" And the blind man said to him, "Master, let me receive my sight." And Jesus said to him, "Go your way; your faith has made you well." And immediately he received his sight and followed him on the way. — Mark 10:47–52

On My Heart

Encounter with Christ

Bartimaeus knocked on Jesus' heart. He asked for mercy, for the Lord's pity, and his prayers were heard. The door was open, he entered, and his eyes were opened. He experienced the healing power of Christ in his life!

Bartimaeus, though unable to see with his eyes, had clear vision of the heart. He opened himself for healing, and we can do the same when we put our faith and trust in the goodness of God. When we ask Jesus for his loving mercy upon us, we may not see physical healing, but we can be assured of spiritual healing.

This encounter is an allegory of our faith journey. As Bartimaeus was cured of physical blindness, we can be cured of our spiritual blindness, making our life with Jesus clearer. Still, it may sometimes take several attempts to become who God created us to be. There is a reason the spiritual life is often compared to a journey. First, we too must cry out to Jesus to have mercy on us. Then, we need to be open to his movement of that mercy in our lives. Though you may want to "cry out" figuratively if you are in Mass or adoration, if you are praying alone, I urge you to feel free to speak (or shout) your desires with bold confidence as Bartimaeus did.

Sitting in the last pew of the adoration chapel, I fought back tears, though I could feel a few rolling along the contour of my cheek. My seeming inability to hold my tongue, especially when I am angry or hurt, had once again landed me in relationship hot water. Why, Lord, am I unable to control my emotions? I felt crushed by the weight of a lifetime of impulsive behavior associated with my ADHD, and contrition welling from the depths of my soul weakened whatever little resolve I had remaining to avoid crying in this public venue. The tears tumbled down upon the Bible resting in my lap. "Lord," I mumbled softly, "please have mercy on me. I don't want to lose any more friends or cause any more family friction."

I used my sleeve to wipe the tear puddles from the cover of my Bible, then mindlessly flipped through the pages seeking comfort and distraction — anything to help me stop replaying recent events on an endless loop in my memory. My eyes rested on Matthew 12:36–37: "I tell you, on the day of judgment men will render account for every careless word they utter; for by your words you will be justified, and by your words you will be condemned." That scared me a little, but it also finally opened my eyes to the truth: I couldn't keep blaming my ADHD when I spoke unkindly to others. But I wasn't on my own with this, either. Jesus would provide me the grace, but I needed to cooperate with it. It was time to embrace faith, be courageous, listen to Jesus, and be healed from my behavioral blindness.

Are there similar blind spots in your life? What do you seek to have your eyes opened to? Jesus' touch, above any temporary physical healing, brings mending and strength to our broken hearts and fragile faith. Just as the people encouraged Bartimaeus, "Take heart; rise, he is calling you," today, I want to offer you the same encouragement. What will you tell Jesus you need? Where do you seek his mercy, pity, and compassion, especially in the ordinary moments of your life?

I often try to take stock of my spiritual wellbeing, giving extra attention to strengthening my relationship with Christ. I look to the examples in Scripture for clues of where I need to grow. In the story of blind Bartimaeus, we see several characteristics we should emulate in our own lives:

- A strong faith
- Persistence in prayer
- Drawing nearer to Jesus
- Acknowledging Jesus as Messiah
- Bold confidence in Christ
- Persistence in spite of the negative opinions of others

Dr. John Bergsma writes of Bartimaeus and his healing:

> Jesus responds to Bartimaeus, "Go your way; your faith has saved you." And Bartimaeus receives his sight! But he does not go his way. He follows Jesus on Jesus's way. That's remarkable. Bartimaeus doesn't just want to have his eyes healed. He wants to be part of the kingdom of Israel that the Son of David is restoring,

> starting with the Twelve New Patriarchs, the Apostles. He wants to be a disciple of Jesus, a member of the Church. We read this account and focus on Bartimaeus receiving his sight. However, there is another lesson on sight going on in the story. The crowd looks at Bartimaeus and sees only a blind beggar, a "throwaway" human being who is not worthy to disturb the busy rabbi from Nazareth. Jesus looks at Bartimaeus, however, and sees a true son of Israel, a victim of the sins of his people and a fallen world. He has compassion on this man and restores his sight and also welcomes him into the New Israel that he is forming around himself: the Church.

Like Bartimaeus, may we approach Jesus with confidence, boldly ask him for what we need, and hear those comforting words, "Go your way; your faith has saved you." And like Bartimaeus, may we choose to follow Jesus in his way, allowing the gift of our healing to draw us closer to him as his faithful disciples.

If we let the spiritual scales fall from our eyes, we may realize how much Jesus cares for each of us. If we view the world with eyes of faith, we can reframe the way we respond to unexpected moments and better see how Jesus provides a way in every situation to move toward some type of health and wholeness. Everyone will eventually die even if healed of some earthly infirmity. Even Lazarus of Bethany, whom Jesus raised from the dead, eventually succumbed to his mortal body and died. So, why did Jesus bother to give sight to the blind, open the ears of the deaf, and restore the use of lame men's legs? To lead us to heaven, and to build in each of us the faith that saves us. Jesus redeemed us by his death and resurrection, and every lesson we glean along the way of life helps us work out our salvation.

Take the sisters from Bethany, Mary and Martha, for instance. When we first meet Martha, she is worried and troubled about a great many things, complaining to Jesus that her sister, Mary, is just sitting at his feet and not helping her serve. Martha has allowed the busyness and the stress of her life to blind her to Jesus' presence. Jesus heals her spiritual blindness when he tells her that her sister has chosen the better part.

Martha takes this lesson to heart.

Amazingly, later in the Gospel of John, after Jesus restores her brother Lazarus from the dead, we read that Mary once again sits at Jesus' feet, this time anointing his feet with oil and drying them with her hair. And once again, we read that Martha is serving. This time, though, there is no more complaining, no more asking Jesus to tell Mary to get off the floor and do something meaningful. Martha now understands that her role is to serve others while her sister, in that moment, is serving the Lord by anointing his feet. No longer blinded by her inward focus, Martha accepts the earlier instruction, not as chastisement but in the caring and loving manner Jesus intended: to help her grow in virtue and holiness. Healed from her blindness, she now serves with a joyful heart.

The most essential effects of physical healing take place in our souls. We're redeemed, yet we live with challenges we must deal with daily. We will remain spiritually blind unless we recognize, acknowledge, and ask to be healed in those broken, ailing, or hurt places in our lives.

An Invitation to Ponder

Blindness can come in many forms. We've all experienced not being able to see, whether in that momentary burn of bright sunlight when you first step outside on a clear day, or in the darkness of a room when you first turn out the light. Most of us have also experienced healing, which can be painful. As the broken places fuse or we learn to use (or reuse) atrophied muscles, there can be major discomfort. Yet thankfully, most often these conditions are temporary. Though it may cause discomfort at first, God can heal our spiritual blindness, and he wants to. But like Bartimaeus, we have to approach him and ask.

In which area(s) of your life do you feel frustrated or even angry without fully understanding the underlying cause — as witnessed in Martha's anger with Mary? Often underneath those icky feelings (which we like to avoid) is a blindness the Lord wants to heal. What devotion or prayer practice do you think you might implement to bring your eyes into clearer focus?

Use the journaling space below to record your answers to these questions and whatever else this reflection has stirred in your heart.

Connecting with Scripture

In this section, I have added five verses for us to reflect upon as we delve further into this chapter's theme on having the faith to cry out to Jesus to heal us and correct our spiritual blindness, trusting that he is ever present, although we cannot see him. Use the space provided to jot down notes and words or even transcribe the entire verse — whatever fosters your prayer and reflection.

Pray: Come, Holy Spirit, guide me as I read and reflect on these Scripture verses and any others you may reveal to me during this time with my Bible. Shower me with all the wisdom, knowledge, and understanding I need to allow your word to dwell in me richly. Amen.

Tobit 2:7–10; 7:7

Psalm 34:17–19

John 9:1–12

. 2 Corinthians 4:17 .

. James 5:7–9 .

Jesus works to remove spiritual blindness, soften hardened hearts, and reunite disconnected communities, bringing each of us a new vision of life in him. When we ask, seek, and knock, Scripture assures us we will have our prayers answered — not necessarily in the way we wish, but always according to God's holy, loving, and all-knowing will. We can trust that, if God chooses not to heal us or our loved ones as we ask, it is because he genuinely has a more incredible, more magnificent blessing prepared for us. Ultimately, he is always working to bring us home to heaven to be with him for eternity.

The *Catechism* expresses it perfectly:

> Prayer *to Jesus* is answered by him already during his ministry, through signs that anticipate the power of his death and Resurrection: Jesus hears the prayer of faith, expressed in words (the leper, Jairus, the Canaanite woman, the good thief) or in silence (the bearers of the paralytic, the woman with a hemorrhage who touches his clothes, the tears and ointment of the sinful woman). The urgent request of the blind men, "Have mercy on us, Son of David" or "Jesus, Son of David, have mercy on me!" has been renewed in the traditional prayer to Jesus known as the *Jesus Prayer*: "Lord Jesus Christ, Son of God, have mercy on me, a sinner!" Healing infirmities or forgiving sins, Jesus always responds to a prayer offered in faith: "Your faith has made you well; go in peace." (2616)

God doesn't bring bad things into our lives, but what he allows, he uses for the good of our souls to bring us closer to him. Much of the bad in the world results from people misusing God's gift of free will — the gift given to us so we might love him. It must hurt his heart to see his children suffering. It can be so difficult to find a reason, feeling like God has abandoned us. Yet we have to trust his words and promises. He will make good from it. He loves us and has not, nor will he ever, abandon us. We discover this truth also in many other passages of the Bible.

I am a goofball; I love to find peculiar tidbits in Scripture that make me laugh. Maybe they aren't supposed to be funny — I admit that sometimes I have the sense of humor of a twelve-year-old — I honestly think sometimes these are the moments God is inviting me to take life less seriously. One particular story that always makes me giggly is the tale of the manner in which Tobit became blind:

> I, Tobit … went into my courtyard and slept by the wall of the courtyard, and my face was uncovered because of the heat. I did not know that there were sparrows on the wall and their fresh droppings fell into my open eyes and white films formed on my eyes. I went to physicians to be healed, but the more they treated me with ointments, the more my vision was obscured by the white films, until I became completely blind. For four years I remained unable to see. All my kindred were sorry for me, and Ahikar took care of me for two years until he went to Elymais. (Tobit 2:9–10)

Of course, it's not funny that Tobit became blind, but the way it happened always catches me off guard. What unexpected circumstances, perhaps even happening in an instant, completely changed my plans or entire life? For instance, when my oldest son was born two months prematurely, my boss closed the business without warning. Or another time, a chance meeting led to a new, beautiful friendship (because not all surprises lead to tragedy or difficulties). For me, Tobit's story leads to an important spiritual reflection: What has blinded me? In what areas of my life am I unable to see? I am often blinded by different things, especially in my spiritual life. My pride, vanity, and insecurity all prevent me from seeing situations clearly, particularly in my relationships. Several friendships in my life have ended because I could not see my role in the conflict — or my selfishness in not allowing others to be who they are and not who I wanted them to be. I encourage you to ask yourself: What blinds you?

Tobit was finally healed after four years of physical blindness. During that time, he waited on the Lord with trust. We see this in his powerful prayer, in which he praises God, saying:

> Righteous are you, O Lord; all your deeds are just and all your ways are mercy and truth, and you render true and righteous judgment for ever. And now, O Lord, remember me and look favorably upon me. (Tobit 3:2–3)

The first step toward any healing is opening ourselves to believing and trusting in God's goodness. God only wills our good and does not bring us evil, though he does sometimes allow it for our sanctification. God provides us the grace to accept our crosses so we can grow in virtue and holiness. Though I know firsthand how challenging that task can be, we can trust that all God does emanates from his sheer, unconditional love for each one of us.

The following may not be a perfect analogy, but it has helped me understand God's fatherly, albeit sometimes confusing, care. I love my kids. When they were little, they really loved candy. Of course, I allowed them to have candy, but there were rules and guidelines around consuming it. These limits were placed out of love. If one of my children came to me at 2:00 in the afternoon and asked for a piece of candy, I'd happily allow it. But for their own welfare I would not allow them to eat twenty pieces. And if my children woke me at 2:00 a.m. asking for a piece of chocolate, again out of concern for their wellbeing, I would not give it to them.

At times, as my children railed against my rules (especially the day after trick-or-treating), I allowed them to indulge in candy to allow the natural consequences to teach where my love could not. God, the perfect

Father, desires what is best for us. His ultimate design for each of his children is for us to be with him forever in heaven, and all he allows into our life, if we cooperate with his grace, can be used to sanctify us and help us achieve this incredible goal.

Let's consider an important lesson about healing that we glean from the story of Jesus' encounter with the man born blind. While it's important for us to ask Jesus for the healing we seek, as Bartimaeus did, sometimes he heals us even without our asking. In this story from John's Gospel, we see Jesus bestowing new sight not only to the blind man, but to all who allow themselves to be healed by the "light of the world" (Jn 9:5).

Living on the margins, reduced to begging to sustain himself, the man born blind may not have even been aware Jesus was present. He certainly did not ask for healing. Yet Jesus, in his loving mercy, chose to restore his sight so that "the works of God might be made manifest in him" (Jn 9:3). This healing, like that of Saint Peter's mother-in-law (whom we will encounter later in this study), is an example of Jesus working to restore faith, moving miraculously, mystically, and momentously in people's lives — even when they don't first ask. And these circumstances in turn are able to awaken faith in others.

In this story, the Pharisees remain blind because they refuse to believe in the miracles that God can do in our lives and the power of Jesus to break through the darkness. The Pharisees believe this man's disability was brought on by his own sin or that of his family. As Jesus shows, there is often no simple explanation for someone's suffering, especially for a disease or disability. Instead, we can trust that God can bring good from all circumstances for "those who love him" (Rom 8:28) and that nothing is impossible for God. In all circumstances, he is still sovereign. It is easy for us to grow weary and to despair. To combat this tendency, we need to cultivate a heart of thanksgiving that remains hopeful. Our sense of what is happening in the world around us, especially when we are hurting or despairing, can blind us, making hope and trust feel impossible. The Pharisees suffered from a powerful spiritual blindness and were unable to see Jesus, the light of the world, standing before them, performing a miracle. It absolutely amazes me that they could witness everything Jesus was doing around them but still could not see that he was the Messiah.

Then I remember I have the gift of hindsight, know of his death and resurrection, yet still have my own moments of suffering from spiritual short-sightedness!

What blinds us, preventing us from seeing the goodness and power of God even when he performs mighty signs right before our eyes? What keeps us in the dark even when we stand before the light of the world? Each of us needs to take time to reflect on this honestly, asking the Lord to heal our blindness — including any blindness we're not even aware of. Jesus came to illuminate our way to heaven, to make clear the path. In order to follow it, however, we need eyes to see. Ask the Holy Spirit to show you your blindness. And trust that, if you ask, the Lord will heal your blindness, just as he healed those who were physically blind in the Gospel.

An Invitation to Share

The Archangel Raphael is the patron saint of healing. The Hebrew word *rapha* is often translated as "healing." Saint Raphael in the Book of Tobit is a messenger and conduit of great healing to Tobit and his family. Compose a short prayer to Saint Raphael seeking his intercession for your own needs and those of your family.

Looking at the characteristics of the blind beggar, which do you feel you possess? Which would you like to grow in? What are some ways you might go about building these dispositions and virtues?

Can you remember a time in your life when a prayer was not answered as you wished, or the response seemed delayed? Using hindsight, what lessons did you learn from how God responded to your prayer? Like my kids who now appreciate my motherly actions when they asked for candy, because they learned how to moderate their sugar intake, what did you learn from God's response to your prayer?

Closing Prayer

Spirit of the Lord, continue the good work begun in me. Grant me the grace to trust you in suffering, especially when I cannot see you at work or feel your presence. Have mercy on me, sending me the grace to hold on to faith even when spiritual sight grows weary and weak. Through my tears, my shouts, even my pouts, illuminate my every step.

Holy Spirit, breathe new life into my every attempt to become who God created me to be, with the faith to weather whatever falls unexpectedly into my life. Help me to look more closely at my desire to please you, opening my eyes wider to see where I can grow in holiness, especially when I fail or fall short. Each encounter with you has helped me better understand why spiritual life is often compared to a journey, bringing comfort to my heart. Sweet Advocate, gather my groanings to perfect them in a prayer for the Lord's mercy to be upon me. Shower me with the gifts of knowledge, wisdom, fortitude, and piety to wipe away any spiritual blindness that remains.

I do not wish to remain a Pharisee, blind to the truth right before my eyes, clinging so tightly to my ideas and agenda that I miss the plan of sheer goodness God has for me. Bid the Lord to call my name, and I will come forward to receive the healing which allows me to draw ever closer to him. This, yes, this alone, is what I long for Jesus to do for me.

FOUR

Reaching Out in Faith

Opening Prayer

Come, Holy Spirit, open my heart and mind to receive the blessings and graces prepared specifically for me in this chapter on the authority of Jesus' healing touch. May I learn to embrace the consolations available when I reach out to Jesus and lean into his promise that he will never abandon me. I long to witness how his heart is moved by an act of sincere faith and touched when I place my hope in him. I long to be like Jairus and the hemorrhaging woman and to reach out in faith!

I yearn to receive the powerful, transforming message of restoration and peace offered throughout the Scriptures. May I learn to approach Jesus with courage, as did the woman suffering for twelve years with a hemorrhage. As I enter this time in prayer, may I put aside all doubt, trepidation, uncertainty, and thoughts of being unworthy to receive the peace you give. Help me to push boldly through all that holds me down or keeps me from a life of freedom in Christ. Gentle Spirit, please loosen anything binding my heart that prevents me from reaching for the hem of Jesus' garment.

Come, Holy Spirit, so I may live in peace, knowing my faith has made me well according to the Father's plan and purpose. May this encounter transform my relationship with Christ, inspiring me to come to believe in his power to make me whole and raise me to new life, just as he did for the hemorrhaging woman and for Jairus's little girl and his entire family. O Paraclete, divine helper, hold tight my hand as I reach out in faith and hope for the healing touch of the Lord.

Encounter with the Word

And there came a man named Jairus, who was a ruler of the synagogue; and falling at Jesus' feet he begged him to come to his house, for he had an only daughter, about twelve years of age, and she was dying. As he went, the people pressed round him. And a woman who had had a flow of blood for twelve years and had spent all her living upon physicians and could not be healed by any one, came up behind him, and touched the fringe of his garment; and immediately her flow of blood ceased. And Jesus said, "Who was it that touched me?" When all denied it, Peter said, "Master, the multitudes surround you and press upon you!" But Jesus said, "Some one touched me; for I perceive that power has gone forth from me." — *Luke 8:41–46*

On My Heart

Encounter with Christ

The Gospels of Mark, Matthew, and Luke each include the interwoven stories of the healing of Jairus's daughter and the woman who suffered hemorrhages for twelve years. The woman's story seems oddly placed between Jairus begging Jesus to save his young daughter, who is dying, and the miraculous raising of the child from the dead. On his way to tend to her, Jesus encounters this unnamed woman. Clearly, these two stories are meant to be forever linked, for there are no mistakes in the Scriptures. I found this commentary by Curtis Mitch and Edward Sri helpful in making sense of this connection:

> From a Jewish standpoint, her stealthily touching Christ's tassel on his cloak would have been disturbing, for according to the law this would make Jesus ritually unclean. From Jesus' perspective, however, this woman exhibited great faith. He looks at her tenderly and says, Courage, daughter! Your faith has saved you. Jesus tells her that it was in response to her faith that he instantly cured her. As in his healing of the leper ... instead of Jesus being defiled by the woman's uncleanness, his divine power transforms her condition. She is healed physically of her ailment, which in turn restores her socially as she is made ritually clean. When Jesus arrives at the official's house, he finds flute players and a crowd making a commotion. This refers to the professional mourners a Jewish family was expected to hire when someone died. Jesus sends them out, saying, The girl is not dead but sleeping. From Jesus' perspective, death is not the last word. Death is like sleep in the sense that there will eventually be an awakening from it. In restoring the girl to life, Jesus demonstrates his authority even over death. He took her by the hand, and instead of becoming ritually unclean through his contact with a dead body, Christ's divine power goes out from him to raise the child from the dead.

It is also interesting to note that the child's age, twelve, coincides with the number of years the woman had been hemorrhaging. I once heard someone speak of the juxtaposition of the innocence and purity of the child with the woman's loss of both through this isolating disease, which rendered her lawfully unclean. The true gift of these two forever-linked stories is the hope of eternal restoration they give to all of us. Learning to turn to Jesus in our time of need brings us from the brink of despair and hopelessness to new life in him. You are important, your soul is of utmost importance — Christ died to prove it.

We can learn from the hemorrhaging woman's faith. Just as he did for her, Jesus allows us to reach out to him — to touch his heart. After nearly twenty years in women's Catholic ministry, I am still astounded by the number of women who have no idea just how precious they are to the Lord. Whatever our reasons may be, we tend to be sadly unaware of the deep, abiding love Jesus has for us. Saint Paul writes, "But God shows his love for us in that while we were yet sinners Christ died for us" (Rom 5:8), proving that God's love for us is never conditioned on our perfection. Moreover, God himself helps us receive his love, as Saint Paul reminds us: "Likewise the Spirit helps us in our weakness; for we do not know how to pray as we ought, but the Spirit himself intercedes for us with sighs too deep for words" (Rom 8:26).

At the same time, while faith is important, I don't want to give the impression that faith automatically heals us, or that not being healed somehow means we're not faithful enough or not praying the right way. God has a plan beyond our comprehension, and his goal is not simply to fix us temporarily (and any earthly healing would be only temporary). He longs for us to be with him in heaven forever. That's his promise, and that's the ultimate plan, which led him to become incarnate and dwell among us. Jesus witnesses to the love of the Father and wants to prepare us for the real healing of eternal life. Eternity is the treasure that this world can neither give nor steal.

In this encounter, we discover a subtle unfolding of a dual meaning of the word *touched* in their exchange. Jesus wants to identify the person of faith who touched him: "And Jesus said, 'Who was it that touched me?'" (Lk 8:45). Courage, maybe fueled by desperation, moved the hemorrhaging woman to seek his help, and he, moved by her faith, seeks her out. The apostles assume Jesus is trying to figure out the source of a physical touch, but I can't help but wonder if he's asking a deeper question, too: "Who has touched my heart with your trust, hope, courage and faith?" Maybe she was motivated by desperation, but whatever moved her, she took the leap of faith to reach out.

And then I wonder, what do I need to reach out to Jesus for — and what fear or doubt holds me back from doing so? Even though I know he desires it, I still worry about reaching out to Jesus. I struggle with this crazy belief that I only get so many prayers answered in my life. Yet the truth is that Jesus is not a genie in a bottle; there's no limit to his love, mercy, and desire to assist me. Even if he does not answer in the way I think he should, he will never leave a prayer unanswered. The hemorrhaging woman is out of options. I know I certainly have found myself in situations where I suffered far longer than I ever needed to out of stubbornness or ignorance, because the answer was always within reach. If I would just reach out to him in faith, I would be able to go in peace, as Jesus instructed the woman.

Perhaps another reason for the interconnectedness of these two healings was to strengthen Jairus's faith. Maybe seeing the healing of the hemorrhaging woman helped him not to lose his own hope and faith in Jesus' divine power. He had to be reminded of the faith that brought him to Jesus in the first place.

Reflecting on this Gospel encounter with Jesus, I'm reminded of a profound experience I had while on a weekend retreat shortly after my reversion in 2009. On Friday, after finishing our program activities for the evening, we all returned to our rooms for some rest. Not long after settling into my room, I heard a strange commotion in the hallway. Barbara, a woman in her eighties who had been allowed on the weekend after a recent lifting of an age restriction on what had once been a young adult retreat, was experiencing symptoms of a heart attack. Other retreatants gathered in the hallway, directing our worry into prayer. In a remarkable "Godcidence," a nurse had decided to attend for the weekend. She stayed with the ailing woman, monitoring her vitals until the ambulance arrived.

In another remarkable indication of the Lord's blessings, the priest on the team had the rare opportunity to stay with us throughout the weekend. (Usually, the priests ministering on the retreat have to leave at the close of the day to attend to parish duties.) As we continued to pray outside Barbara's room, Father Joe administered the anointing of the sick. The snowy weather and remote location of the retreat house, which caused a tremendous delay in the ambulance's arrival, only added to the drama of the moment.

As we prayed and Barbara's condition worsened, with no sight of the ambulance, I could feel my panic and anxiety begin to build. The ambulance did finally arrive, but sadly, Barbara would pass away in the hospital later that evening. For the rest of the weekend, I battled crippling anxiety.

Although there were indications of God's providence at every step, my anxiety-blindness reigned supreme. Finally, late on Sunday afternoon, I chose to hand the three days of near-constant panic and anxiety over to

Jesus. The turning point came when it was my turn to pray for the session speaker. As I knelt before the tabernacle in our small makeshift chapel, I noticed that the bottom of the gold tabernacle strongly resembled fringe. I thought of the story of the hemorrhaging woman. In her desperation, she had mustered what strength she had left and resolved to press her way through the crowd to seek the healing power of Jesus. Overcoming what had to be tremendous fear, she reasoned that if she could just get close enough to brush against the hem of his garment, the twelve years of being unclean and outcast would end. She had spent all she had seeking a cure through earthly physicians; her only remaining option was the Divine Physician.

Summoning my courage, I reached out and touched the molded gold along the bottom of the tabernacle. As my fingers lay upon the cold metal, peace coursed through my body for the first time in days, and I believed, without a shadow of a doubt, that Jesus' power had been unleashed in me. Jesus, moved by compassion as he had been for the woman who was healed after twelve years of exhausting every route of healing, had healed me. Why did I suffer so long in that panic and anxiety before bringing it to him and seeking his help and his healing? May the woman's courageous example move us all to lay aside any hesitations or fears we may have, and to reach out to Jesus, the one Physician whose healing touch never fails us.

An Invitation to Ponder

One subtle, underlying theme of the hemorrhaging woman's story is lamenting lost time. Seeking a cure for her illness dominated twelve years of this sick woman's life. Her willingness to risk becoming a permanent outcast in her community, or even worse, to receive healing from Jesus, illustrates the desperation and despair her circumstances rendered. Do you ever wrestle with regret over lost time or missed opportunities? In Revelation, we hear God remind us, "Behold, I make all things new" (21:5). How can your faith help you see those lost moments as redeemed? How can you move forward from this moment in hope and peace?

Use the journaling space below to record your answer to these questions and whatever else this reflection has stirred in your heart.

Connecting with Scripture

In this section, I have added five new verses for you to reflect on to further your understanding of this chapter's theme of recognizing the authority of Jesus' healing touch. Use the space provided to jot down notes and words or even transcribe the entire verse — whatever best fits your prayer and reflection.

Pray: Come, Holy Spirit, guide me as I read and reflect on these Scripture verses and any others you may reveal to me during this time with my Bible. Shower me with all the wisdom, knowledge, and understanding I need to allow your word to dwell in me richly. Amen.

Psalm 103:2–4

Matthew 8:5–13

Luke 7:1–10

2 Corinthians 4:16–18

Hebrews 11:4–16

Faith is one of the theological virtues (hope and charity are the others, for those who may be wondering). All three of the theological virtues "are infused by God into the souls of the faithful to make them capable of acting as his children and of meriting eternal life" (CCC 1813). Faith is the undeserved, free gift of God's Holy Spirit, the "virtue by which we believe in God and believe all that he has said and revealed to us, and that Holy Church proposes for our belief, because he is truth itself" (1814). Faith is an essential element for hoping (or trusting) in God's will for us, and for developing a deep abiding love for him — reciprocating the love he already has for us.

We see this theme of faith woven throughout the Scriptures on healing. Jesus frequently acknowledged people's faith before, during, or after moments of healing. Yet I do want to offer a word of caution here: When we or someone we love is not healed as we ask, this does not necessarily mean we lack faith; God's will is a mystery. The psalmist illustrates that faith in the Lord comes with many benefits, which can include healing our diseases. But other benefits are forgiveness, redemption, God's crowning us with love, and many more. We may not always receive the healing we seek, but it is important to approach Jesus with faith, especially during our time with him in Mass.

In the story of the healing of the centurion's servant (see Mt 8:5–13 and Lk 7:1–10), we may recognize words similar to those we recite in every Mass during the Liturgy of the Eucharist as we prepare to come forward to receive Our Lord. When Jesus tells the centurion, "I will come and heal him," the man responds, "Lord, I am not worthy to have you come under my roof; but only say the word, and my servant will be healed" (Mt 8:7–8). During Mass we declare, "Lord, I am not worthy that you should enter under my roof, but only say the word and my soul shall be healed." I know I am guilty of making this a perfunctory response rather than really praying the words during Mass. I say the familiar words, but after years of repetition and a daily battle against a lukewarm spirit, I do not contemplate the deeper, awe-inspiring meaning of the words I parrot along with my fellow communicants.

Both Luke and Matthew recount this story of Jesus healing the centurion's beloved servant. In Luke's Gospel, Jewish elders come to Jesus on the Roman official's behalf, which speaks volumes about the man's character. "And when they came to Jesus, they begged him earnestly, saying, 'He is worthy to have you do this for him, for he loves our nation, and he built us our synagogue'" (Lk 7:4–5). In both Luke's and Matthew's retelling of this encounter, we hear the centurion profess his unworthiness for Jesus to enter under his roof, along with his recognition that Jesus' words hold immense power. The Roman centurion of Capernaum, as a man of authority himself, respected and understood, at a profound level, something many of us will spend a lifetime never genuinely comprehending about Jesus. Jesus wields sovereignty both in heaven and on earth; his word, which spoke everything into being (Jn 1:3), reaches wherever he chooses it to reign.

In Matthew's account (see 8:5–13), pay close attention to Jesus' response to the centurion's declaration of faith in his authoritative power to heal without physically being present to the centurion's distressed servant: "When Jesus heard him, he marveled, and said to those who followed him, 'Truly, I say to you, not even in Israel have I found such faith'" (v. 10). The *Catechism* tells us, "Jesus is as saddened by the 'lack of faith' of his own neighbors and the 'little faith' of his own disciples as he is struck with admiration at the great faith of the Roman centurion" (2610).

If the pagan centurion's testament of faith was so powerful, how much more significant is the moment in Mass when we followers of Christ declare our unworthiness to receive this same Jesus under our roof? Jesus is truly present in the Eucharist, which means we encounter him in his healing power in this sacrament. I was reminded of this reality when I read this powerful statement from Dr. Mary Healy:

> In the Eucharist, we encounter Jesus and Jesus is the healer. … So

> if we receive the Eucharist in faith — and we should keep in mind that *Eucharist* refers to the entire Eucharistic liturgy, not just the consecrated host, but the whole gift of the Holy Mass, of gathering with God's people to have made present to us again the sacrifice of Christ on the cross, which is the source of all healing, and then to receive him into our very bodies as the medicine of immortality — if we receive in faith, it cannot help but be healing.

How often do we come to Mass with our minds distracted by worries or concerns, or our hearts heavy with burdens? We are, in a word, distressed! The centurion's faith sent him to the one place, the one man he knew could relieve his distress. He came to Jesus, but he also understood this proximity was not necessary for Jesus to unleash his divine power. In the Mass, we have the opportunity to receive Jesus, truly present in the Eucharist — Body, Blood, Soul, and Divinity. We bring our prayers and petitions to him, and then we leave the church, but we are called by faith to understand that Jesus remains with us and can continue to answer our prayers, heal our distress, and provide us the strengthening grace necessary to undertake our earthly journeys.

As I've said throughout this book, not every prayer for healing is answered as we might wish. But sometimes the Lord does amaze us with the gift of recovery. A woman at church, whom I only knew by sight and the smiles we exchanged during the sign of peace, once approached me and asked me to pray for her, as she'd recently been diagnosed with breast cancer. I don't typically do this, but I felt very strongly that the Holy Spirit was prompting me to pray for her at that very moment. She immediately knelt before the authentic replica of Our Lady of Guadalupe in our parish.

A year later, she came up to me with tears in her eyes, proclaiming that she had been found cancer-free after treatment. She shared, "Jesus just wanted to save me. He healed me, and I confessed I was sorry for being so far away from him. Jesus has become my best friend, and I no longer care about my bank account or material things. I just want to be close to him." She further shared that she had begun to feel that way even before she realized she was cancer-free. He carried her through the entire ordeal, and she was so grateful for the chance to see how far away she had grown from him, even though she attended Mass every week.

The story of the centurion also reminds me of Venerable Patrick Peyton's miraculous healing from tuberculosis. The young Pat Peyton was suffering from advanced TB and was given two options for treatment: a very risky operation on his lungs or prayer. As he considered the dangerous procedure, his friend Father Cornelius Haggerty came to visit, and they shared a powerful interaction, which Father Patrick describes in his autobiography, *All for Her*:

> "You have the faith, Pat," [Father Cornelius] said, "but you're not using it. You brought it with you from Ireland. Your mother gave it to you, just as her mother had given it to her." He dwelt on that point, recalling a passage in which St. Paul describes how the faith is transmitted from mother to son. Then he explained to me how meaningful prayer to Our Blessed Mother would be, if only I used the faith I possessed. "Our Lady will be as good as you think she is," he said. "If you think she is a fifty per-center, that is what she will be; if you think she is a hundred per-center, she will be for you a hundred per-center. No one of us ever does as much as he is capable of doing. We always fall short, stopping on the near side of our total effort." It was startling to be addressed in such words, but not nearly as startling as what he said next. "Even Our Lord and Our Lady do not do as much as they could do," he added, "but the reason is that we think they are not able. We limit them by the extent of our faith." Then he made me another wonderful statement. "I will begin a novena of Masses for you tomorrow, and that's the greatest thing on earth. It is not just some holy man or some holy woman praying for you for nine days. It is Jesus Christ praying to His Father for you. And that is power infinitely greater than any power on earth."

The young seminarian, who desired nothing in life more than to finish his studies at Notre Dame seminary and become a priest, turned to the Blessed Mother and began to pray in earnest for her intercession in his healing. With Our Lady's prayers, Pat began to miraculously recover from his deadly diagnosis.

After he was healed, Venerable Patrick Peyton turned this gift of grace into a mission. After his ordination, he prayed for a way to repay the Blessed Mother's intercession, but more importantly, to find a way to serve the Church and her Son in accordance with God's will. He would eventually establish Family Rosary, the Rosary Crusades (speaking to millions of people about the power of family prayer, especially the Rosary), and later in life, Family Theater Productions. What a testament to using the gift of new life to serve others with gratitude and thanksgiving!

In Hebrews 11, we see what power faith can have in a person's life. Saint Paul provides a very long list of people who accomplished the impossible by their faith. While our faith does not always change the circumstance, nor can it alter the outcome, especially when we are surrendering to God's good and perfect will, prayer changes us and the way we see the situations we find before us. How easy it is to have faith when we receive what we pray for. How much more amazing are those whose faith remains unwavering even when their prayers are not answered according to earthly expectations!

An Invitation to Share

We can all identify at least one person in our lives who has been afflicted in one way or another, yet continues to cling to faith and never lose hope. Which characteristic do they embody that you would like to emulate? How does their story inspire you to trust in God's perfect, yet sometimes confusing, plan for your life?

Have you ever felt punished by God when something bad happens in your life? Does learning that God always has a plan of sheer goodness for your spiritual wellbeing help mitigate those feelings or fears?

What situation is currently stealing your joy? Are you plagued by comparison being the thief of your joy? Take a quick survey of your blessings, and all the ways you can (or maybe already do) glorify the Lord with your life.

Closing Prayer

O Divine Helper, inspire within me the courage necessary to reach out to Jesus with faith as I conclude this chapter on the healing touch of Christ. Open my heart and mind to embrace the blessings and graces revealed within these pages. Please help me discover the power of reaching out to Jesus, the ever-present, ever-loving Divine Physician.

Although my crosses can feel heavy and overwhelming, continually remind me, beloved Paraclete, that Jesus' healing power is just a fingertip, a prayer, or a glance away. What joy to know Jesus is always so close that it is not hard for me to reach him — and he, me! I may have to push through the craziness and distractions of my life to reach him, but Jesus promises to always be found by those who seek in faith and hope. When I draw near in faith, I will always be given the power to rise again — restored, renewed, redeemed.

Come, Holy Spirit, into my heart so I may encounter the life-giving, compassionate power and touch of Jesus. May I recognize that the Divine Physician longs to have us come to him in faith, hope, trust, and love to mend our broken places. Please send an outpouring of your grace into my hemorrhaging places so that I may be healed! Protect me from growing weary in prayer. Sustain me always in the peace this world cannot give.

FIVE

Believing It Can Be Done

Opening Prayer

Come, Holy Spirit, open my heart and mind to receive the blessings and graces God has prepared specifically for me in this chapter on humbly seeking healing and believing that Jesus does will it for me. Miracles still happen even if they come disguised as a renewed sense of peace or patient acceptance of my circumstances. May this encounter transform my relationship with Jesus, and may I come to believe he never ignores my pleas, especially when I approach him with sincerity and deference, submitting myself to his sheer goodness.

May I encounter Jesus with the openness to beg for the scraps from his table of plenty. May I pray with conviction, knowing that as unworthy as I feel, I am precious in his sight. As a beggar for grace, I fall at Jesus' feet pleading for mercy, especially for those conditions in my life that have become chronic — both physically and spiritually. Holy Spirit, prepare my heart to be willing to accept even the minutest favor of your gratuitous love.

Wise Counselor, please loosen anything binding my heart, clouding my mind, or causing me to withdraw rather than finding the comfort and peace Jesus has come to offer me. Teach me to approach Jesus with the heart and posture of the "grace beggar" I am. Please hear my meek and desperate pleas for Jesus' cleansing touch and outpouring of mercy. Whatever the Father wills, Sweet Spirit, embolden my heart to accept it with joy.

Encounter with the Word

And a leper came to him begging him, and kneeling said to him, "If you will, you can make me clean." Moved with pity, he stretched out his hand and touched him, and said to him, "I will; be clean." And immediately the leprosy left him, and he was made clean. — Mark 1:40–42

On My Heart

Encounter with Christ

The Gospels of Matthew, Mark, and Luke are called the Synoptic Gospels. *Synoptic* means "with one eye," and these Gospels are referred to in this way because they are all closely linked. Each Gospel writer spoke to a different audience, so while they share many of the same stories, they do so in slightly different ways. Matthew, the tax collector, was one of Jesus' apostles. He spoke to a Jewish audience focusing on the fulfillment of the Messianic prophecies. Mark, believed to be the John Mark discussed in the Acts of the Apostles chapter 12, was a scribe, and we believe that he transcribed and recorded the teachings and memories of Peter. Mark was also a companion of Paul and Barnabas and spoke to a Roman audience. Finally, we have Luke, the physician. Luke's audience was Greek. It is also clear that he, too, had conversations with the Blessed Virgin Mary, as his Gospel is the only one that includes details of the birth of Jesus.

The three Synoptic Gospels offer us a beautiful opportunity to view some of the most significant moments in Jesus' earthly ministry from three unique perspectives. These three Gospel writers either personally witnessed these events or heard firsthand accounts from people who watched these historical moments unfold. And each of these writers draws our attention to different aspects of the encounter with Jesus. It would be the same if we heard about the same event (for instance, a wedding) from different people. The bride's friend would remember her dress, facial expressions, and her parents' reaction as she said her vows. The priest would be much more focused on the magnificent rite for which he was privileged to stand in the place of Christ. Both recollections of the glorious day would be true and accurate depictions. Still, they are not likely to be identical, and that is beautiful because together, they give a much broader view, filling in the details. Such is the case in the Gospels when Matthew, Mark, and Luke (and sometimes John) recount the same event.

So as we read about the healing of the leper in Matthew 8:1–4, Mark 1:40–45, and Luke 5:12–16, we discover both similarities and unique nuances in this story of healing. I encourage you to read each of these versions of the story yourself, noticing how each portrays this powerful moment of healing.

The leper who seeks healing in this story exhibits a pattern of behavior that we can emulate as we approach Jesus for assistance in whatever ails, isolates, or disturbs us. First, our posture: Two of the Gospel writers depict the leper as kneeling, while another describes him dramatically falling on his face. Our posture in prayer is important, whether we're standing, sitting, kneeling, or falling down prostrate upon the ground, begging for the Lord's mercy.

The words the leper and Jesus exchange show us the importance of humility when we approach the Lord. The leper is unassuming yet undoubtedly desperate as he begs, "If you will, you can make me clean" (Mk 1:40). Each of the Synoptics records Jesus' verbal response the same way: "I will; be clean" (Mk 1:41; Mt 8:3; Lk 5:13). Yet the descriptions of the physical healing Jesus grants differ slightly. I am particularly interested in Luke's rendition, since he was a doctor himself. Luke describes Jesus stretching out his hand and touching the leper. This is significant for several reasons. I will touch (pun intended) on two: First, Jewish law stated that anyone who touched a leper would himself be made unclean. Jesus reached out and touched the leper anyway. This exchange reminds me of a moving encounter I had with a Franciscan priest many years ago at a conference. He introduced himself and reached out his hand to shake mine, like so many people do. Since my eczema flare was at one of its worst states, I recoiled my hand and nodded a greeting instead. Feeling his confused expression deserved an explanation, I showed my hands to this kind priest and apologized for not being able to accept his polite gesture. In an instant, and much to my utter amazement, this young man gently took my hands and kissed them. "Do not be ashamed or hide your hands. They do not extinguish the beauty and dignity the Lord bestows upon you as his beloved daughter."

Second, the Scriptures often portray Jesus healing with touch. This laying on of hands to bring healing harkens to the rite offered in the Sacrament of the Anointing of the Sick. In this sacrament, the priest anoints the sick person with oil on the forehead and hands, saying, "May the Lord who frees you from sin save you and raise you up."

Jesus' response to the leper in this story, as one would expect, is loving, swift, and gentle. Hearing the humble man's plea for help, he heals him with a touch. Jesus is moved with pity for the man's condition. His heart is touched by the man's need and his humble request. Jesus' response is immediate. Cleansing this man of his illness not only restores his health but also allows the man to return to the community from his life of isolation. God wants each of us to live in communion with others, as we are created in his image, and he himself is a loving communion of three divine Persons — Father, Son, and Holy Spirit. The devil seeks to divide us from one another and from ourselves, while the Lord, the Prince of Peace and Truth, reconciles and heals, lovingly mending our broken places, restoring our communion with one another, and making us whole again.

Scripture scholars Edward Sri and Curtis Mitch describe this encounter between Jesus and the leper:

> The man suffering with leprosy exhibits amazing faith. He already believes Jesus possesses the ability to heal him, but in his humility he implicitly asks whether Jesus wills to exercise his divine power to make him clean. He also shows Jesus great reverence. The man did him homage and called him Lord. The most

> astonishing part of this encounter, however, is Jesus' response. Jesus has the ability to heal from afar (see [Mt] 8:8, 13), yet he chooses to touch the man whose leprosy makes him ritually unclean. From a Jewish perspective, this contact should have rendered Jesus himself ritually unclean. But here, the opposite occurs: Jesus' holiness transforms the uncleanness of the man suffering leprosy and makes him clean.

The leper approached Jesus with the posture of humility, both physically (kneeling or lying prostrate) and spiritually (with a beggar's heart). Jesus' reputation had preceded him, but most likely this poor man had never encountered the Lord before this moment. The leper exemplifies the willingness to trust in what cannot be explained, to hold with hope and trust the teachings of Christ, believing he is who he says and can do what he promises. Perhaps distress and anguish motivated the leper's actions, but Jesus saw his heart and granted his prayer to be made clean. Thus, we can conclude faith, even if it is as small as a mustard seed, resided within him.

For three years, I battled dyshidrotic eczema, a condition with painful blisters and peeling skin, which made my hands feel unclean and untouchable. It isolated me and left me feeling like a leper. Like the lepers described in Leviticus 13:43–46, I felt like I should put on a shirt emblazoned with the words, "Unclean! Unclean!" as a modern-day version of wearing torn clothes, covering my upper lip, and crying out those words to all who approached me. This isolation was a constant source of anxiety and self-doubt. I turned to prayer, pleading with God to heal me, but my prayers seemed to go unanswered. I wondered if I was praying hard enough, if I lacked faith, or if I had somehow angered God. The persistent nature of my condition made me question God's love and mercy. Yet ultimately, through this experience, I learned valuable lessons about patience, humility, and the enduring love of God.

Then, when I least expected it, the Lord reached down from heaven through the hands of a holy priest. Fr. Ubald Rugirangoga was from the Cyangugu diocese of southeastern Rwanda. During the 1994 genocide, Fr. Ubald lost over eighty members of his family and over 45,000 of his parishioners. He escaped through the Congo on foot in the middle of the night. Eventually, he returned to Rwanda to preach healing, forgiveness, and reconciliation.

Thousands came to his healing Masses in Rwanda and additional services worldwide. He was renowned for countless healings of every kind. In 2018, I had been suffering for three years with this exhausting and debilitating skin disease. Fr. Ubald surprised the conference team on which I was serving with a private healing service. Always optimistic that God would eventually heal me and knowing Fr. Ubald's reputation, I lined up to be prayed over and have him lay his hands upon me. As his hand engulfed the top of my head, a wave of warmth traveled through my body. A calm peace filled my heart. It would have been enough if that were my only gift at that moment.

I went back into the conference hall to see if there were any tasks I could do, even with limited use of my hands. Moments later, two of my dear friends, who had traveled with me to assist and experience the powerful retreat, came rushing through the door. Father Ubald had just offered a closing reflection and prayer, in which he named the healings the Lord performed through him that evening. "He said someone's hands have been healed. He had to mean you, he had to!" They were so excited that they spoke over each other. I responded with, "From your lips to God's ears." Unlike the leper from the Gospels, my healing would not be instantaneous. However, it would be miraculous, and so complete that no one would ever guess how deformed my hands once were.

Another biblical leper, Naaman, was healed from leprosy by the prophet Elisha (see 2 Kgs 5:1–19). After his cure, this pagan expressed his gratitude to God and vowed to worship him alone. We also learn about the power of gratitude to deepen our relationship with God from the ten lepers in Luke's Gospel, all of whom were healed by Jesus — yet only one returned to thank him. My ongoing journey with dyshidrotic eczema is a challenging one, but it has led me to a deeper understanding of faith, patience, and gratitude. I have learned that even in the darkest times, God's love and mercy are present — that he does desire to heal me, just as he willed to make the leper clean.

The leper in this story teaches us the proper disposition with which to approach Jesus, both physically and mentally. This includes prayer; unwavering (even wavering) trust that Jesus is who he says and can do even the impossible; and a heart filled with gratitude at the goodness of God. When faced with debilitating situations of any sort, we too have the choice to humbly seek the Lord for help and healing. Whether on our knees or prostrate on the floor imploring Jesus' assistance, our prayers should emerge from a place of hope, patience, and gratitude. Only through prayer can we ourselves reach a place of receiving Jesus' promise, "I will; be clean."

An Invitation to Ponder

Can you recall a time you felt like an outcast? Have you been faced with a chronic condition of your heart, mind, soul, or body in which you felt no one truly understood your struggle? Did you ever bring this condition to Jesus to beg for his assistance in removing or carrying the cross with you?

Use the journaling space below to record your answers to these questions, as well as whatever else this reflection has stirred in your heart.

Connecting with Scripture

In this section, I have added five new verses for you to reflect on to further your understanding of this chapter's theme of humbly seeking healing and believing that Jesus does will it for you. Use the space provided to jot down notes and words or even transcribe the entire verse — whatever fosters your prayer and reflection.

Pray: Come, Holy Spirit, guide me as I read and reflect on these Scripture verses and any others you may reveal to me during this time with my Bible. Shower me with all the wisdom, knowledge, and understanding I need to allow his word to dwell in me richly. Amen.

Psalm 40:1–13

Mark 7:26–30

John 10:10

2 Corinthians 1:2–4

Galatians 5:18–23

Psalm 40 begins, "I waited patiently for the Lord; / he inclined to me and heard my cry. / He drew me up from the desolate pit, / out of the miry bog, / and set my feet upon a rock, / making my steps secure." Oh, King David, you had me at "miry bog"! These places often lack oxygen, are difficult to traverse, and can literally bog you down. How do we land in these metaphorical desolate pits? Sometimes we fall in unaware, other times we are seemingly pushed in by the actions of another, and sometimes we jump in with both feet through our choices or decisions. Regardless of how you find yourself mired in a spiritual bog, there is nothing to compare to the joy found in raising your hands to heaven and having the Lord lift you from this dark, cold place and set you securely back on solid ground.

The Lord does not seek burnt offerings and sacrifices, but a heart that hopes in him, trusts in his goodness, delights in doing his will, and believes in his holy promises. As we read in Mark's Gospel (7:26–30), with eyes of faith, we cannot miss Jesus' presence with us. The Syrophoenician woman (a woman from the region of Tyre and Sidon, which is located in present-day Lebanon), demonstrates persistence in faithful prayer in seeking Jesus' blessings. At the same time, this encounter reveals Jesus' willingness to listen to every plea regardless of our background, social standing, or current spiritual state.

Before Jesus encounters the Syrophoenician woman, we read in Mark's Gospel, "And he entered a house, and would not have any one know it; yet he could not be hidden" (7:24). Consider this subtle, powerful statement. Does Jesus go unnoticed in your home? Are you able to ignore his presence in your life?

The Syrophoenician woman's faith ("yet even the dogs under the table eat the children's crumbs") teaches us that even the scraps from Jesus are enough to heal. The very least that Jesus has to give us could transform our lives. Imagine if we embraced even a tiny bit of the blessings and graces that Jesus has to offer us — how would our lives be changed? At the same time, the gifts available from heaven are abundant, so we do not need to settle for the crumbs, though even they alone would still be enough to fill us. Our lives would not be perfect or free from those things that worry, concern, or pain us, but there would be an inner peace and hope that can only come from heaven.

The woman came to Jesus prepared to be persistent, humbled, and assured. Her persistence was evident by her begging and her humility in addressing him as Lord, willing to take whatever scraps he offered. She believed what he had said was done because she left for home at his command. When was the last time I approached Jesus in that way — begging for assistance, humbled by his majesty and glory, and yet utterly sure that I would somehow receive a blessing, the one he knew I needed?

What are the demons you need Jesus to drive out from your life? Do you struggle with insecurity, anxiety, uncertainty, maybe an addiction, a complicated relationship, or a financial crisis? How remarkable that even the slightest grace from Jesus, the scraps from his table, can transform our lives. Imagine the possible freedom awaiting us if we embraced even a tiny bit of the blessings Jesus offers us.

Dr. John Bergsma helped me make better sense of this somewhat odd, even awkward, exchange between the Syrophoenician mother and Jesus. He explains:

> Jesus adapts his way of dealing with people to their individual situations and needs. … We need to understand Jesus's actions as tailored to the faith of this woman. He sees that she has faith — he puts her faith to the test to elicit more faith. Untested faith is no faith at all. "It is not right to take the food of the children and throw it to the dogs," Jesus says — a painful reminder that Gentile pagans have no covenantal claim on the God of Israel, no right to call him to be faithful to his obligations toward them (*hesed*), only the ability to throw themselves (ourselves!) on the mercy of God the Creator. The woman has both tremendous faith and tremendous humility. Not taking insult from Jesus's words, humbly acknowledging her lack of any covenant claim on the God of Israel, she asks for unmerited mercy: "Please, Lord, for even the dogs eat the scraps that fall from the table of their masters."

What holds us back from being fed by Jesus? Feeling, perhaps, unworthy of even the crumbs from his table? How can the Syrophoenician woman's example encourage us to approach Jesus for assistance in casting out whatever demons we need to eradicate from our lives?

The Holy Spirit wants to help us discern those things that keep us from allowing God to work in our lives. In his Letter to the Galatians, Saint Paul exhorts us to embrace a life in the Spirit, to seek grace, which is the undeserved gift of God living within us. The Spirit animates us from within, enabling us to imitate Christ — not by our doing, but by his power within each of us. Sadly, we often seek healing for our physical ailments, but we forget that there are remedies for our spiritual ailments as well.

We look after our spiritual wellbeing, first of all, by growing in awareness of what the Lord calls us to avoid. If you want to prepare a really thorough confession on your next visit to the sacrament, spend some time sitting with Saint Paul's laundry list of works of the flesh found in Galatians 5:19–21. This is a fascinating look at the different behaviors Jesus calls us to avoid for our spiritual good. While it can be painful to recognize and admit these things about ourselves, it is a crucial element in the healing process and essential for our sanctification.

As we gradually remove the works of the flesh from our lives, we will also begin to see the fruits of the Spirit flourish (see Gal 5:22–23). These fruits reflect the love and life of Christ through us. It is so easy to forget about the third Person of the Trinity and his role in our spiritual wellbeing, yet Jesus has sent him to us to help us live as he taught us. The *Catechism* teaches, "By this power of the Spirit, God's children can bear much fruit. He who has grafted us onto the true vine will make us bear 'the fruit of the Spirit: … love, joy, peace, patience, kindness, goodness, faithfulness, gentleness, self-control' (Gal 5:22–23). 'We live by the Spirit'; the more we renounce ourselves, the more we 'walk by the Spirit' (Gal 5:25; cf. Mt 16:24–26)" (CCC 736).

Heaven is only for the pure. We cannot stand before God's majesty with even a speck of sin upon us. This is sobering, but we also have the assurance that God never asks the impossible; our loving God never sets us up to fail or perish. He is too merciful and loving for that. Through the Scriptures and traditions of our faith, God imparts remedies to help us work out our salvation and claim the redemption his Son won for us on Calvary. We can also be assured this is the cleanliness the Lord will always will for us!

And one last thought on suffering: God never wastes our pain. As Saint Paul reminds us, when we allow Christ to comfort us in our trials, we learn to be Christ to others. Read Paul's words very slowly and thoughtfully, especially if you are currently knee-deep in a miry bog: "God of all comfort, who comforts us in all our affliction, so that we may be able to comfort those who are in any affliction, with the comfort with which we ourselves are comforted by God" (2 Cor 1:3–4). Maybe you've already experienced the joy of how sharing your story blessed, comforted, and encouraged someone else as they trudged through the same mirky, oxygen-deprived circumstances you once trod through. Sharing the same healing we have received is yet another way Jesus wills to make us clean!

An Invitation to Share

Where have you seen Jesus at work in your life recently? Did you recognize him, or did you need someone to point out his handiwork to you? In what new ways can you tune your spiritual barometer to stay focused on all the ways and places he can be found in your life?

In telling the story of the leper, I chose to include all three of the Synoptic Gospels because sometimes seeing things from multiple angles clarifies our understanding or perspective. Recall a time when listening to another person's retelling of a story or situation broadened your awareness or increased your empathy.

Consider Saint Paul's message that if we allow God to be our comfort through trials and tribulations, we'll be blessed to do the same for others. Share any moments when you've experienced this in your life. How might you be proactive in using those past (or even current) lessons associated with your afflictions to comfort others in a similar situation?

Closing Prayer

O Holy Spirit, I know you will continue the good work you have begun in me during this chapter on humbly seeking healing and believing that Jesus does will it for me. I do believe Jesus has more abundant blessings to offer me than I could ever imagine. I am overwhelmed by gratitude for Jesus' constant presence in my life, for his calling me to the banquet of his goodness and grace. And whether I am at the table for the feast or at his feet for the crumbs, help me, Spirit of God, to always be assured I will never be without his unending blessings and graces.

So many circumstances remain unresolved; I wish for the strength to surrender them and experience the true peace and consolation only Jesus offers. Protect me, Spirit of Truth, from the world's lie that the bad that befalls me comes from God's wrath, and from the false promises that comfort can be found in any place but faith. Help me to accept the love and the perfect will that the Father has for my life. Whatever the suffering, regardless of how long I am called to endure it, help me to believe that my prayers are heard and they will be answered. Whether the answer is yes, no, or not yet, may I continue to glorify you with the Father and the Son, and to share the many ways I experience moments of faith in my life.

May I continue, daily, to encounter Jesus' restorative, cleansing power and love in my life, just as the leper and the Syrophoenician woman and her daughter did.

SIX

Would You Witness, Serve, or Speak?

Opening Prayer

Come, Holy Spirit, enlighten my heart and mind to receive the blessings and graces prepared specifically for me in this chapter on rising after Jesus speaks his power into my distress, responding with grateful service and glorifying God by telling every ear willing to hear. Healing comes in so many ways. Please help me not to miss you at work in my life. Help me to consider how I respond in times of wellness and strength, as well as in weakness and struggle. May I always witness to Jesus in the world around me.

As I read and reflect on the Scriptures in this chapter, O Spirit of Enduring Hope, I bring before you the many people and circumstances that vie every day for my attention and care. Help me see that all the other pieces in my life will fall into place if I put you first. Quiet my mind, filled with tasks, concerns, and responsibilities. Help me instead to focus during this time on the living, dynamic word of God. Do not allow me to continue to put off spending time in prayer; instead, please guide me to find daily time at the feet of Jesus, beginning now.

Come, Holy Spirit, so I may clearly hear Jesus' gentle reminder that when I make him my priority, I never have to navigate this life alone. I desire to build a genuine and intimate relationship with you by the gift of your dwelling in me through my baptism. Help me to find balance and peace. May this encounter transform my relationship with the Father, the Son, and with you, Spirit of Truth. May I come to believe time spent in prayer is always the better part of what I need to do each day, just as Martha did on that busy day in her home. Like Peter's mother-in-law, may I also rise and serve with a grateful and joyful heart.

Encounter with the Word

And he arose and left the synagogue, and entered Simon's house. Now Simon's mother-in-law was ill with a high fever, and they asked him about her. And he stood over her and rebuked the fever, and it left her; and immediately she rose and served them. Now when the sun was setting, all those who had any that were sick with various diseases brought them to him; and he laid his hands on every one of them and healed them. And demons also came out of many, crying, "You are the Son of God!" But he rebuked them, and would not allow them to speak, because they knew that he was the Christ. — Luke 4:38–41

On My Heart

Encounter with Christ

The healing of Peter's mother in law is one of the Gospel stories that appears in all three of the Synoptic Gospels. All three include Jesus' healing touch, the woman's fever that left immediately, and what happened next: She rose and served. After her healing, many sick and possessed people were brought to Jesus for healing. It is unclear why Jesus was at Peter's house, but many scholars seem to agree that it was just part of the ordinary course of his life at this time. Perhaps he stayed there often, so it would have been routine to retreat to Peter's home for a meal and some rest after spending time in the synagogue.

I've always been amused by Peter's mother-in-law's response to being healed. Although I understand the theological teaching, as a mother who occasionally enjoys milking an extra sick day (you know, the day *after* you start feeling better), I never understood why she didn't take a day or two to rest before she started working again. I guess, like Martha of Bethany, Peter's mother-in-law had learned to imitate Jesus and had taken his teachings to heart. So, when she was restored to health, her immediate reaction was to imitate him and serve others.

Jesus surprised the apostles with the humble and powerful message, "even as the Son of man came not to be served but to serve" (Mt 20:28). As a witness not only to Jesus but also to Peter's living out this mission, this woman's actions would then become a hint to how we can use our lives to carry out whatever mission God gives us, especially in the service of others and the care of our world. Unselfishly tending to the needs of others and putting others first are in themselves life-giving and healing.

In Luke's account (remember, Luke was a physician), Jesus *rebukes* the fever — the same word we will see later to describe how he deals with the demons. Scripture scholar Pablo T. Gadenz explains the connection between the fever and the casting out of demons:

> Jesus rebuked the fever as he had "rebuked" the demon (4:35) (a detail not found in the synoptic parallels), indicating that the two miracles should be considered together. Illness, whether physical or psychological, is very different from demonic possession (see *Catechism* 1673). The oppression caused by evil spirits can, however, have harmful effects on the body, as indicated later in the story of the crippled woman (13:11, 16; see *Catechism* 395). Moreover, illness, with its ultimate consequence, death, is an evil from which Jesus the "physician" (4:23) liberates human beings. In this case, again in response to Jesus' powerful word, it left her. The verb here is *aphiēmi*, related to the "liberty" (*aphesis*) proclaimed by Jesus "to captives" (4:18). … The healing occurs immediately (see 5:25; 8:44, 55; 13:13; 18:43). She got up or, more literally, "she arose" (*anistēmi*) … the same verb used later for

> Jesus' resurrection (18:33; 24:7, 46). Like Jesus and because of Jesus, his followers will experience a resurrected new life, as the woman did. In gratitude, she waited on them. Her response is one of service (see 8:3), by which she also imitates Jesus (22:27).

Let's look at what happens after Peter's mother-in-law is healed. Each of the Gospel accounts has a tiny difference in word use that I think is worth considering. Each Synoptic writer shares that the people who came had various illnesses, and these included not just physical but spiritual ailments, with many needing to be freed of demons. Jesus laid his hands upon the afflicted to bring healing. In Luke's rendition, he says every one of them was healed. Jesus leaves no prayer untouched or unanswered, whether or not his answer is what we originally sought. We can be assured that our encounter with Jesus will not leave us the same.

In Matthew's account of the healing, all the sick who were brought to Jesus were healed. Mark uses the word *many* when referring to the number of people who received healing. Perhaps Matthew (the tax collector — a numbers guy) had a more accurate accounting, or maybe the language has a more profound message. It is not that Jesus couldn't heal everyone; I am sure everyone who came to him believing and seeking was indeed healed. Yet we know that not everyone who prays for healing receives a clean bill of health. On the other hand, many who need Jesus to heal them will not ask. Sadly, they never see a need for his saving power in their lives. When we refuse to ask Jesus to heal us, we allow the demons of doubt, fear, ignorance, or arrogance to block the grace available in Jesus' healing touch.

Peter's mother-in-law had a fever, and Jesus healed her. Jesus has healed me in so many facets of my life. He's filled empty crevices and crevasses with hope, love, joy, and abundant gifts of grace. He has granted me recovery from physical afflictions, some rather miraculous, but those pale in comparison to the gratitude and joy I experienced when Jesus healed my spiritual, emotional, and mental wounds.

Sometimes, because God always answers my prayers according to his plan and not mine, the answers differ from my spoken request. I have often begged Jesus to remove certain thorns of chronic illness, yet they remain. Saint Paul speaks about a thorn in his side, which he asked God three times to remove, yet it remained (see 2 Cor 12:1–10). It remained to protect Paul so he would boast only about what God did in his life and not fall into pride or forget he could do nothing without God.

The line from the hymn "Amazing Grace" — "I once was lost, but now am found" — could be sung about anyone who has said yes to following Jesus. Even those of us who are already faithful followers of Jesus have moments where we need to come closer and be healed. But like Saint Paul, we all have also suffered thorns we've begged the Lord to remove, and he has not done so. When we surrender our will and accept our circumstances, we can experience the freedom that comes from not being healed but still loving the Lord. We accompany him as faithful disciples — simply for the hope of heaven.

It is also interesting to note that in many of the healing stories in the Gospels, Jesus strictly tells those healed to tell no one (see Mk 1:40–44; 7:36; 8:29–30; Mt 16:20; Lk 9:20–21). Certainly, Jesus knew his hour to redeem the world would come soon, and his mission was not simply about attracting people who wanted healing of their bodies. Far more importantly, he came to prepare our hearts and minds for his true mission of redemption — neglecting neither mind nor soul with his teachings, and even with the miracles he performed.

Some of the people Jesus healed listened to him and kept quiet. Others ignored him and talked about their healings to anyone who would listen. I relate to the latter group of blabbermouths. At the risk of sounding ridiculous, I never worry about appearing as a fool for the sake of spreading the Good News. How can I keep what God does in my life to myself? It's too remarkable, and honestly, I struggle with the desire to share too much; I'm the queen of "TMI." I would love to share such a story related to the adoption of my daughter Faith from China.

Many years ago, we discerned that the Lord was inviting us to adopt a child. In the early stages of discernment, I was very nervous about how I would know which child God meant for us. Returning to prayer, especially before the Blessed Sacrament, I felt the Holy Spirit reveal that my child would be deaf, and she would be three years old. I so believed this prophecy that I began learning American Sign Language and told everyone about it. I knew that when the Lord fulfilled what he had told me, I would glorify him through the story. Although I would tell people I could be wrong, I knew the prophecy was true and wanted to tell them about it anyway, so they would see how amazing our God is when he fulfilled it. Despite my conviction, we did not search only for three-year-old children who were deaf. On the adoption application, we circled many special needs that we were open to accepting.

Finally, on April 30, 2009, we received the long-awaited phone call from our adoption agency, saying they'd found a child who was a perfect match for us. The agency shared what we'd known all along: The little girl was three years old and profoundly deaf. Even crazier, as her emailed photo popped up on my computer, I couldn't help but giggle at the resemblance between this beautiful little girl from China and my middle child of Portuguese and French descent. It was a resemblance only the Lord could arrange! People would often remark after she came home that she looked just like us. I love how the Lord answers our prayers and heals our doubts and fears; when he does, how can we keep it to ourselves?

An Invitation to Ponder

Prayer is the root of all healing and the essential component for our encounters with Christ to bear fruit in our lives. Consider how you incorporate prayer into your daily life. Prayer as a vehicle for communicating with Jesus can't be sporadic if we truly want to be in relationship with him. Do you have relatives you only see on holidays or at funerals and weddings? How would you characterize your relationship with them? Is that the kind of relationship you want to have with Jesus? If not, what simple changes (like finding a space with no distractions) can you make to build in more prayer time and strengthen your friendship with Christ?

Use the journaling space below to record your answers to these questions and whatever else this reflection has stirred in your heart.

Connecting with Scripture

In this section, I have added five new verses for you to reflect on to further your understanding of this chapter's theme of rising after Jesus speaks his power into our distress, responding with grateful service, and glorifying God by sharing what he has done for us. Use the space provided to jot down notes and words or even transcribe the entire verse — whatever works best in your prayer and reflection.

Pray: Come, Holy Spirit, guide me as I read and reflect on these Scripture verses and any others you may reveal to me during this time with my Bible. Shower me with all the wisdom, knowledge, and understanding I need to allow your word to dwell in me richly. Amen.

Psalm 100.

Matthew 6:5–15

Philippians 4:4–7

1 Timothy 6:11–16

James 1:5–8

Sadly, I think I can count on one hand the times I've held the disposition of thanksgiving expressed by the psalmist, "Enter his gates with thanksgiving, / and his courts with praise! / Give thanks to him, bless his name!" (Ps 100:4). It is especially difficult to have this attitude when I am suffering, but embarrassingly, I am not sure I even show the Lord the proper gratitude when I am in times of consolation or peace! I know this primarily stems from my lackadaisical prayer practices. I'm so stubborn when it comes to changing my ways and making time for the Lord. Instead, I continue to sleep later in the morning instead of making time for Jesus before leaving for work. My failure to embrace this mindset of gratitude and routine of prayer means I don't receive the fruit that I know emerges from my prayer — not only for myself, but also for others!

The apostles were slow learners like me, which is probably why I love them all so much. They give all of us consolation and hope that the Lord can work with us even in our weakness. In Matthew's Gospel (6:5–15), we read of a private discussion between the apostles and Jesus, when they ask him to teach them how to pray. He instructs them to make time, away from the busyness of life, just as he modeled for them (and us) again and again during his ministry on earth. In the Lord's Prayer, he then gives them the words that will help them communicate clearly, humbly, and lovingly with God the Father.

In the Lord's Prayer, we proclaim our faith in God as our Father, acknowledge the holiness of his name, hope for the Kingdom of God, and seek the grace to submit to his perfect will. We also recognize our need for God's protection from temptation. Jesus taught the apostles to rely on God for their daily needs. This prayer would take on another level of meaning when he became the Bread of Life for us in the Eucharist. In this prayer, Jesus reminds us of his mercy and forgiveness and how we are to keep our hearts open and prepared to receive this mercy by being merciful to others.

These words shared with the apostles two thousand years ago, which allow us to see into the intimate conversation between the Father and Son, are a precious gift. The words of this prayer should tumble from our lips and hearts every single day! I invite you to take extra time with this passage from Matthew's Gospel this week, really studying how Jesus himself taught his apostles (and us) to pray. God's fatherly love and devotion to us are what will allow us to grow in holiness, especially as we navigate difficulties and respond to blessings.

I had a conversation with my son not too long ago to apologize for always trying to make things better when he was a child. I hate the term "helicopter mom," but sadly for me, the cliché fits! I couldn't resist swooping in and trying to save him from ever feeling disappointment or loss. Instead, I inadvertently robbed him of opportunities to deal with difficulties on his own. My love for him led me to try to protect him, but in the end, I did more harm than good. The good news is that he still loves me, accepts my apology, and understands my motivations came from a place of great love.

I often think about the parenting techniques of God, who is our loving Father. If I need to allow my child to feel suffering, to learn how to live with struggles, in order to build his coping skills and strategies, how much more does God do that. After all, he's a much better parent than I am!

The Lord is indeed good and merciful. Our response to every breath we take, which we know stems from him, should be one of thanksgiving and praise. This attitude of gratitude not only acknowledges God's goodness but also fosters a deeper sense of appreciation and reverence in our hearts. And it makes us ready, like Peter's mother-in-law, to rise and serve the Lord when he gives us the gift of healing.

Prayer is the root of all healing, as well as a means to discover a peace that surpasses all our human understanding. My spiritual director once gave me excellent advice when I complained of feeling dry in my prayer and, as a result, just "off" in my daily life. He suggested I find a place in the house that offered me the least amount of distractions. That choice was easy for me, but not so pleasing to my husband, as I chose his office. Nothing in that room belongs to me, so it is easy for me to cozy up on the little sofa we placed in there, click on the fake fireplace, light a candle, and give my full attention to Jesus. I love my morning "coffee with Christ" time, and it truly has transformed not only my prayer life, but every other aspect of my life as well. I love this reminder about the healing power of prayer from the *Catechism*, especially in relation to those whose stories we are discovering in this study:

> Prayer to Jesus is answered by him already during his ministry, through signs that anticipate the power of his death and Resurrection: Jesus hears the prayer of faith, expressed in words (the leper, Jairus, the Canaanite woman, the good thief) or in silence (the bearers of the paralytic, the woman with a hemorrhage who touches his clothes, the tears and ointment of the sinful woman). The urgent request of the blind men, "Have mercy on us, Son of David" or "Jesus, Son of David, have mercy on me!" has been renewed in the traditional prayer to Jesus known as the *Jesus Prayer*: "Lord Jesus Christ, Son of God, have mercy on me, a sinner!" Healing infirmities or forgiving sins, Jesus always responds to a prayer offered in faith: 'Your faith has made you well; go in peace'" (2616).

Holiness begins as a gift of grace, but it flourishes through our faithfulness to prayer and living the Christian life, particularly through participation in the sacraments and study and reflection on the Scriptures. Prayer, Sacraments, and Scriptures, which I have dubbed the "Grace Trifecta," have become my secret formula for growing in holiness. In Philippians 4, coincidentally the first Scripture passage I ever memorized, Saint Paul gives us a formula for prayer, especially when experiencing any type of anxiety in our life. With joy and thanksgiving, share what is on your heart, hand it over to the Lord and leave it with him, then allow his peace to wash over you and remain with you. Repeat these steps as often as you need; Saint Paul would tell you do so without ceasing (1 Thes 5:17). Approaching God in humble prayer, frequently participating in the sacraments, and delving daily into God's word, all with a disposition of thanksgiving, is where you discover the abundant grace of God.

Grace is that critical component that helps us embrace peace regardless of our circumstances, health, finances, etc. In all things, this begins in prayer, which opens us to receive the grace Jesus wants to give us. Then we have to live out the grace we are given, asking God, as Saint James says, to give us wisdom. When I wake up every morning and make time for prayer and spiritual reading, I find I possess that outpouring of grace necessary to cooperate with God's plan for my life.

Here's a silly but perhaps helpful example of the grace we can receive when we cooperate with God, specifically the spiritual gift of wisdom in the face of temptation: I'm allergic to dairy and gluten. I can't eat them, I shouldn't eat them, and I am usually strong enough to avoid them. Yet I am also a mortal being who really loves ice cream, especially the cherry dip vanilla ice cream from Dairy Queen. It makes me sad every time I drive by, knowing I cannot eat it because it makes me sick. As the heat of the summer wears on each year, my resolve dissolves, and at least once a year I give in and gleefully down the small cup of deliciousness. And each year, I regret it.

This is where asking God for wisdom comes in, and it is very critical to have the proper, virtuous attitude toward the healing power of Jesus in our lives. It is the invaluable outcome of prayer that helps me cooperate with my condition and the grace of God, thereby avoiding the suffering — discomfort, fatigue, and irritability — that succumbing to temptation brings me. To be clear, eating ice cream is not a sin, and I am not sinning against God by indulging in my favorite summer treat. I merely offer this as an analogy for deeper reflection on what it looks like for us to cooperate with grace. For years, I prayed for these bodily responses to be healed. When the cause of my sickness was revealed (dairy and gluten), I still didn't want to do what I needed to remain healthy, and I slipped more often than I care to admit.

Yet the beauty is when we, through prayer, surrender to grace instead of trying to fix ourselves through our own sheer will, we find comfort, healing, and hope. And it is in these moments, the ones that bring us through the storm or help us ride the waves, that we receive the grace not only of healing for ourselves, but to bless others as well. Fight the good fight of the Faith, remaining steadfast in battle, so you may receive whatever healing the Lord has in store for you and then discover how you are called to rise and serve, with thanksgiving and, I pray, renewed hope!

An Invitation to Share

As I mentioned, I have always been amused by Peter's mother-in-law's response to being healed. What was your initial response to this Scripture story? Share what your response would have been if you had been in her situation and Jesus healed you.

Do you have a "coffee with Christ" time that you can set aside each day? Where can you carve out a set place in your calendar to be refreshed, strengthened, and renewed in your faith and friendship with the Divine Physician? How can you ensure this is one appointment you never skip, postpone, or avoid?

Have you ever asked for wisdom from God for big (or little) decisions in your life? If yes, what were those decisions, and what was the outcome? Heeding Saint James's advice for anyone who lacks wisdom, take some time to reflect on areas in your life now where an outpouring of wisdom would be helpful and ask God for it.

Closing Prayer

Come, Holy Spirit, open my heart and mind to receive the blessings and graces you have prepared specifically for me in this chapter on rising after Jesus speaks his power into my distress, encountering healing, responding with grateful service, and glorifying God by telling every ear willing to hear. O Spirit, who raised Jesus from the dead, and now through my baptism lives also in me, rebuke any evil spirits that threaten to steal my joy, hope, and faith. Restore me to a place where I can serve my Lord and share the Good News with others.

Father, Son, and Holy Spirit, fill me so that I can wholeheartedly and without reserve love and trust you. You know my struggle to love and trust people physically present in my daily life; without your palpable movement of grace within my life, I fear I will falter in faith. Yet I believe you never ask the impossible; in fact, the Scriptures remind us, "With men this is impossible, but with God all things are possible" (Mt 19:26). With this powerful truth in mind, I turn toward heaven and vow to remain open to receive the abundant yet unseen gifts you have prepared before the beginning of time for me.

Spirit of Knowledge and Understanding, I long to know the many gifts of God — faith, grace, joy, and eternal life, to name only a few. Enable me to tell my problems how big my God is, instead of allowing my situations to deceive me into collapsing inward in despair. May a prayer be ever on my lips, the sacraments incorporated into every day, and Scripture the lamp before my every step. May this encounter fill me with wisdom and transform my relationship with Christ, helping me come to believe in his healing power. May I use the gifts of healing I have received to give of myself in service, just as Peter's mother-in-law did.

SEVEN

Still Healing Today

Opening Prayer

Come, Holy Spirit, open my heart and mind to receive the blessings and graces prepared specifically for me in this chapter on the many ways Jesus continues to heal in the world today and how we continue to be changed by our daily encounters with him through prayer, Scripture, and, most powerfully, the sacraments.

I am so grateful for the efficacious grace available to me in the seven sacraments — for the outward sign of your grace in every aspect of my life. Please, our Advocate and Comforter, help me embrace the healing, transformative, and guiding grace available daily through my baptism and confirmation, in my vocation, and in regular reception of the Eucharist and reconciliation. Please open my heart and mind to recognize how you use each of these means to accompany me along my earthly path.

Come, Holy Spirit, inspire my heart to desire regular encounters with Christ, especially through receiving the Eucha-

rist and participation in reconciliation. Help me to fully accept and use every good and perfect gift available by grace, including all the virtues and every merit and grace I receive. Spirit of the Lord, open the eyes of my heart to recognize with reverent awe and wonder how Jesus humbled himself to be truly present to me in the guise of bread and wine and in the Church's priestly servants. Help me comprehend that every encounter with you makes me better and holier than before.

Encounter with the Word

Jesus said to them again, "Peace be with you. As the Father has sent me, even so I send you." And when he had said this, he breathed on them, and said to them, "Receive the Holy Spirit. If you forgive the sins of any, they are forgiven; if you retain the sins of any, they are retained." — John 20:21–23

On My Heart

Encounter with Christ

The risen Lord showed his apostles great mercy, even after they abandoned him in his greatest hour of need, running and hiding in fear. Only St. John the Evangelist (along with some of the women) remained and stood at the foot of the cross. However, Jesus' greeting as he stands among the apostles after his resurrection from the dead is not a chastisement. Instead, he tells them, "Peace be with you" (Jn 20:19). Jesus demonstrates the limitless power of his mercy as he breathes the Spirit upon them, conferring the authority to forgive sins. In yet another way, this action fulfills the words Jesus spoke at the Last Supper as he washed their feet: "For I have given you an example, that you also should do as I have done to you" (Jn 13:15).

The mercy Jesus offers us in the Sacrament of Reconciliation is transformative. The *Catechism* provides this magnificent explanation of the grace available in confession: "Interior repentance is a radical reorientation of our whole life, a return, a conversion to God with all our heart, an end of sin, a turning away from evil, with repugnance toward the evil actions we have committed. At the same time it entails the desire and resolution to change one's life, with hope in God's mercy and trust in the help of his grace" (1431).

A "radical reorientation of our whole life" seems powerful language for what happens when we enter a confessional and lay out our offenses before the priest, who acts *in persona Christi* (in the person of Christ). Can't I simply bring my laundry list of "should haves" and "should not haves" directly to Jesus in prayer? Why involve a middleman? Many people wonder this, yet there are profound reasons for participating in this sacrament, in which Jesus chooses to offer us his love and mercy through his priestly minister.

There was a time when I was petrified of the Sacrament of Reconciliation. My heart raced, my palms grew sweaty, my throat closed, and my feet wanted to sprint to the nearest exit. Honestly, I avoided it until the Holy Spirit nudged me to go, and over time, he overcame my fear.

The Sacrament of Reconciliation always provides us with a genuine encounter with Christ, who is eager to impart grace and wash away our iniquities and cleanse us from our sins (see Ps 51). We have the assurance that Jesus told his apostles, "If you forgive the sins of any, they are forgiven; if you retain the sins of any, they are retained" (Jn 20:23). He wants us to experience his mercy through his ordained ministers, to whom he has entrusted this deeply important work. Sure, it can be uncomfortable; that's contrition! Yet Jesus teaches that the kingdom is now, and we enter it through the Church he established — with her priestly ministers, sacraments, devotions, and abundant graces.

As for that middleman? I am grateful for the opportunity to encounter Jesus through the priest because I have yet to experience anything in this world as sweet as the words he says at the end of each confession: "The Lord has freed you from your sins. Go in peace."

My initial "reversion" focused on the Sacrament of Reconciliation, mercy, and healing. It happened by accident, if I am honest. After a rather traumatic split from a tight-knit church friend group, I needed a change of scenery for Mass. My husband and I returned to the church where we first met, and I began attending a Saturday adoration hour. That hour happened to coincide with the weekly confessions at the parish. As the

Lord often does in my life, he answered my prayer for healing and a restoration of my brokenness through what I thought were coincidental circumstances. The Sacrament of Reconciliation is one of the sacraments of healing (along with the anointing of the sick); somehow, like many aspects of my Catholic faith, I had missed that little nugget in my catechesis.

My heart was in pieces after the loss of my group of friends. Confusion reigned in my thoughts as I wrestled with trusting God again. I was confident he had brought me these friends of faith in answer to a prayer. Then everything went amuck. They left the Catholic Church, and I found sustaining the friendship extremely difficult, even painful at times. How could I heal and mend my broken heart and shaky faith? Of course, the answer was through him. Only through grace can we accept that there are things we just will not be able to understand this side of heaven. Trusting God doesn't mean receiving explanations and clarity, but the wisdom to believe that anything he allows in our lives he promises to use for our good, our sanctification, if we cooperate with him to that end.

My transformation didn't happen overnight (such change rarely does). But in one sweet moment sitting before Jesus in the Eucharist, I realized that whatever he willed for me, I wanted — as scary as those words can be. And furthermore, I knew that when I stepped into that confessional, I was genuinely encountering Jesus in his priest. One cold, snowy month just after my friend group fell apart, I went to confession three weeks in a row. I went each week because I was in the church already for adoration, and I didn't want the priest to have come over for confessions only to have no one enter the confessional. As it turns out, what I thought was a favor for others was the very thing my shattered soul needed to be glued back together by grace.

Over time, as I returned to the confessional for a refilling of grace, I came to recognize where I shared responsibility for the divisions and heartbreak among my former friends. Releasing those bitter roots can be some of the most painful yet most cathartic blessings when we open ourselves to Jesus for healing!

Saint Thomas, sometimes called "Doubting Thomas," is the only apostle who was missing during the first incredible encounter of the apostles with the Risen Christ. Jesus came to the upper room to meet his friends and offered them his peace. Thomas, who was not there, struggled to believe when the others told him about it. He demanded signs and wonders, physical evidence to open his eyes to the truth. I think all of us can sympathize with Thomas's doubt at some point in our lives. Sometimes, it can be hard to remember that we live in Jesus' victory over sin and death now. We are not waiting for it to happen in some future state. At the same time, we are those who, as Jesus told Thomas, have not seen and yet believe — and while it can be difficult, we have Jesus' assurance that we are blessed (see Jn 20:29).

We must take care not to diminish the wonder and awe of Jesus' life, death, and resurrection. Abundant graces flowed from Jesus' side on that dark afternoon on Calvary, and they are ours for the taking, if we will just receive them. Sadly, too often we continue to choose darkness, instead of emerging into the light of Easter. We remain stuck in Good Friday because of sin. The Sacrament of Reconciliation gives us the chance — again and again — to start living in our heaven now. Because if we wait for it, we may miss the opportunity altogether.

In confession, we encounter Christ in a real and personal way, to be cleansed of our iniquities and strengthened with the grace to go forth and sin no more. Although we will fall again, the grace that we receive in the sacraments empowers us to resist temptation and seek God over the things of this world. Made right with God through this sacrament, we experience an outpouring of God's mercy. I experienced this in a profound way once, when I was specifically asking the Lord for physical healing.

There is a reason the medical field refers to hypertension, or high blood pressure, as the silent killer. Most people who suffer from it, yours truly included, have no idea there is anything wrong. If it weren't for a video conference with my Catholic Mom team to record our New Year's podcast, I may have never known the severity of my heart condition. As we chatted following the recording, I noticed the carotid artery in my neck flickering rapidly. Scanning the other women's necks, I quickly realized this wasn't normal, and probably was not a good sign. When my husband arrived home a few minutes later, I had him take me directly to the emergency room. My blood pressure was 184/104! Even after an hour of resting and deep breathing, it remained quite elevated; miraculously, I did not have a stroke and knew I'd been given a second chance to be well.

Ironically, I had been praying a novena for good health and wellbeing as my plate overflowed with amazing opportunities and work for the Lord. After the ER visit, I kept thinking, *Jesus, I want to hear you tell me all will be well, that I will have this chance to complete all these good things.* Then, I began the desperate search to hear those words from him, randomly opening the Bible every day hoping I'd flip to that exact page, or waiting in anticipation during Mass to hear some word of comfort just for me in the day's readings. Neither happened.

Then I had a profound encounter with Jesus in the Sacrament of Reconciliation. Sitting with Father Harrison, truly one of the holiest, gentlest, and kindest priests I am blessed to know (and I know a lot of them), I was ready to receive what the Lord wanted to give me in the sacrament. For the first time since my emergency room high blood pressure incident, I was present in the moment, just listening — present for this healing encounter with Christ. Then it happened. As I prepared to recite my Act of Contrition, Father prayed out loud, "Lord, may this woman know your desire to complete the good work you have begun in her."

My sobs burst forth, and I laughed through my smeared mascara as I searched my purse for a desperately needed tissue. It was not so much the words that pierced my heart and brought the outflow of tears as much as the circumstance. In the Sacrament of Reconciliation, the priest sits in the place of Christ — *in persona Christi*. My prayer to hear those words directly from Jesus had been answered, and although it would take a few months before I saw physical restoration in my body, in that minute, I knew I'd been graced with spiritual healing.

Prayer, receiving the sacraments, and reading Scripture: I've found this is the perfect prescription — the panacea that cures all my ills. Following our doctor's orders (taking our medicine, proper nutrition, getting exercise) typically results in the healthiest outcome for our bodies. How much more will we enjoy strong spiritual health if we listen to and obey the Divine Physician? Sure, none of us is perfect in our quest for physical health and wellbeing, but it doesn't stop us from trying (or at least learning about what we need to do) to improve our health. Let us consider the benefits of applying that same mindset to building our spiritual muscles, following the Divine Healer's prescription and guidelines for our souls.

So maybe this is a stretch, but this is how my cute little brain works. One day, at the height of the eczema flareup on my hands, I began to notice remarkable similarities between the eczema on my hands and the sin on my soul. Both required specialized treatment — to heal my hands, the remedies included changing my diet, finding the proper hand cream, and at times, taking medication. For the healing of my soul, I needed a daily examination of conscience, stillness to allow the voice of God to penetrate my busyness, and, most importantly, the Sacrament of Reconciliation.

Here are just a few of the connections I made between my ailings and my failings:

- The root cause of the ailment or sin may not always be immediately evident; it can lie dormant within us for years before something triggers its eruption to the surface.
- To eradicate the illness or the frequent fall from grace, one often needs to examine it from all angles, especially from within. We may have to x-ray the inner workings to discover the course of action necessary to be free from disease and discomfort, whether physical or spiritual.
- Healing, whether physical or spiritual, may come with moments of pain, embarrassment, or dismay, and it can create anxiety as we wait for the antidote to take effect.
- In order to be properly healed, we need to present ourselves to the physician (in the case of spiritual healing, to the Divine Physician, Jesus, in the person of a priest).
- The longer we put off that visit, the sicker we become, and the harder it may become to find help, meaning we cause ourselves to endure unnecessary suffering.

I often felt embarrassed and ashamed of my hands and would hide them, much like being caught in the shame or guilt of sin and wanting to hide it from God. Yet covering up (either my illness or my sins) does no good in bringing about healing. Aside from seeking the professional help of a doctor, one of the most recommended treatments for my eczema was to expose my skin to the healing properties of the sun. As I mulled this skin and sin analogy, I couldn't help but see one more connection, with the play on the words *sun* and *son*. On a spiritual level, that is, the Sacrament of Reconciliation, I expose myself to the healing remedy of grace from the Son, which radically transforms my soul, healing my spiritual brokenness and making me whole again.

I have focused on the Sacrament of Reconciliation in this chapter, but I also want to touch on the anointing of the sick — another powerful sacrament of healing. The Bible describes how the apostles "anointed with oil many that were sick and healed them" (Mk 6:13). Saint James further clarifies this in his letter: "Is any one among you suffering? Let him pray. Is any cheerful? Let him sing praise. Is any among you sick? Let him call for the elders of the Church, and let them pray over him, anointing him with oil in the name of the Lord; and the prayer of faith will save the sick man, and the Lord will raise him up; and if he has committed sins, he will be forgiven" (Jas 5:13–15). What strikes me about these passages is how they help clear up the misnomer of "last rites," long associated with this sacrament of healing. Of course, the oils are not a magic elixir, nor are the words of the rite an enchanted spell. As with all sacraments, these are merely outward signs of the inward reality of the outpouring of efficacious grace.

In the *United States Catholic Catechism for Adults*, we read:

> The Rite of Anointing tells us there is no need to wait until a person is at the point of death to receive the Sacrament. A careful judgment about the serious nature of the illness is sufficient. … When the Sacrament of Anointing of the Sick is given, the hoped-for effect is that, if it be God's will, the person be physically healed of illness. But even if there is no physical healing, the primary effect of the Sacrament is a spiritual heal-

> ing by which the sick person receives the Holy Spirit's gift of peace and courage to deal with the difficulties that accompany serious illness or the frailty of old age.

Additionally, I want to offer a word of caution and an exhortation to please not wait until the final moments of a loved one's life to reach out for a priest. With the growing priest shortage, you cannot always be guaranteed one will be readily available. It is also good to get those graces early so the person can lean on them as they navigate their illness, surgery, or those final days. Also, don't just call upon this beautiful sacrament for the dying. Avail yourself of the anointing before undergoing a surgery, or while navigating treatment for a difficult diagnosis, such as cancer. In my mind, seeking to receive this sacrament equates to emulating all the incredible people we've encountered in this study to boldly, humbly, in faith and hope, approach the Lord for his healing touch.

For the last word on this, I want to refer to Pope Benedict XVI and his 2007 papal exhortation *Sacramentum Caritatis* (The Sacrament of Charity), where he describes so beautifully the connection between healing and the Eucharist, especially in relation to the anointing of the sick. He writes:

> Jesus did not only send his disciples forth to heal the sick (cf. Mt 10:8; Lk 9:2, 10:9); he also instituted a specific sacrament for them: the Anointing of the Sick. … If the Eucharist shows how Christ's sufferings and death have been transformed into love, the Anointing of the Sick, for its part, unites the sick with Christ's self-offering for the salvation of all, so that they too, within the mystery of the communion of saints, can participate in the redemption of the world. The relationship between these two sacraments becomes clear in situations of serious illness: "In addition to the Anointing of the Sick, the Church offers those who are about to leave this life the Eucharist as viaticum." On their journey to the Father, communion in the Body and Blood of Christ appears as the seed of eternal life and the pow-

er of resurrection: "Anyone who eats my flesh and drinks my blood has eternal life and I will raise him up on the last day" (Jn 6:54). Since viaticum gives the sick a glimpse of the fullness of the Paschal Mystery, its administration should be readily provided for. Attentive pastoral care shown to those who are ill brings great spiritual benefit to the entire community, since whatever we do to one of the least of our brothers and sisters, we do to Jesus himself (cf. Mt 25:40).

An Invitation to Ponder

How is Jesus close to you in the sacraments? Try to recall your experience with as many of the sacraments as you can. Keep in mind that the graces of the "one-and-done" sacraments (baptism and confirmation) remain with us forever. How do the gifts you received in those sacraments continue to help you grow in faith?

Take a moment to reflect on the beauty, power, and grace that are abundantly available in the seven sacraments of the Catholic Church. Use the journaling space below to record your answers to the above questions and whatever else this reflection has stirred in your heart.

Connecting with Scripture

In this section, I have added five new verses for you to reflect on to further your understanding of this chapter's theme on the many ways Jesus, risen from the dead, continues to heal in the world today, and how we continue to be changed by our daily encounters with him through prayer, Scripture, and most powerfully, the sacraments. Use the space provided to jot down notes and words or even transcribe the entire verse — whatever fosters your prayer and reflection.

Pray: Come, Holy Spirit, guide me as I read and reflect on these Scripture verses and any others you may reveal to me during this time with my Bible. Shower me with all the wisdom, knowledge, and understanding I need to allow his word to dwell in me richly. Amen.

. Psalm 51 .

. John 19:25–27 .

John 20:19–23

Hebrews 6:4–8

Revelation 21:1–5

Psalm 51, one of the seven penitential psalms, includes the beautiful petition, "A clean heart create for me, God; / renew within me a steadfast spirit" (v. 12, NABRE). I encourage you to spend time reading this full psalm. It is a fabulous way to prepare one's heart for the Sacrament of Reconciliation (or to reflect on along with any penance the priest has assigned after your confession). King David composed the psalm as a plea for mercy after he committed adultery with Bathsheba and then arranged for the death of her husband on the battlefield. It is referred to as the *Miserere*, or Prayer of Repentance. In spite of his great sin, God would later describe King David as "a man after my heart, who will do all my will" (Acts 13:22).

This concept of spiritual cleansing and renewal calls to mind the care of a physical wound that, unless thoroughly cleaned and tended to, becomes infected and possibly even septic. As the skin and tissue work to renew themselves, there can be discomfort, maybe even pain, and there is a need to be vigilant in caring for the wound throughout the healing process. The Catholic Church is, as Pope Francis described her, "a field hospital that takes in the weakest people: the infirm." Her most efficacious remedy is offered through the seven sacraments, particularly the sacraments of healing.

Following the Resurrection, in what is sometimes referred to as *John's Pentecost*, Jesus appears to the apostles and bestows upon them the authority to forgive sins, "'Peace be with you. As the Father has sent me, even so, I send you.' And when he had said this, he breathed on them and said to them, 'Receive the Holy Spirit. If you forgive the sins of any, they are forgiven; if you retain the sins of any, they are retained'" (Jn 20:21–23). Through the beauty of apostolic succession, the priest in the confessional, acting *in persona Christi*, says, "*I* absolve you from your sins" (not "*God* absolves you from your sins"). This is because the priest is acting as Christ at that moment. What a tremendous gift to come before Christ, bare our souls with all their broken and tattered pieces, and be made whole again through a mercy we cannot begin to truly comprehend!

These graces are always available to us, but we must constantly seek them out and pray for the grace to remain steadfast in faith even in times of great suffering. In times of illness, hardships, or tragedy, it can be easy to believe that heaven has abandoned us, leading us to turn away from our faith. The words of Hebrews 6:4 — "For it is impossible to restore again to repentance those who have once been enlightened, who have tasted the heavenly gift, and have become partakers of the Holy Spirit, and have tasted the goodness of the word of God" — offer us a sobering warning. Staying close to the sacraments, especially the Holy Eucharist and reconciliation, fills us with grace, an ever-important element of faith that helps us stay close to God in all circumstances. Although the writer of Hebrews warns of its impossibility to return, this author is living proof of Jesus' reminder that "with men it is impossible, but not with God; for all things are possible with God" (Mk 10:27).

So, how do we maintain hope and continue to lean into the sacramental graces found in the Catholic Church? We stay connected to God, our faith, the Church, and others navigating the same path by participating daily in prayer, making time to reflect on the word of God, and participating in the sacraments, which includes calling upon the grace of our baptism and confirmation, and, if we're married, of matrimony. Additionally, we take Jesus up on his generous offer to give us Mary as our mother.

Every word spoken by Jesus from the cross took every ounce of energy he had left and caused excruciating pain. Crucifixion was a brutal ordeal, and Jesus would have had to press down on the nails in his hands and feet as his only point of leverage to elevate his body in order to breathe — or speak. While every word he ever spoke held unfathomable significance, those final words spoken in his three hours upon the cross should be given extra attention, including the gift of Mary as our mother: "But standing by the cross of Jesus were his mother, and his mother's sister, Mary the wife of Clopas, and Mary Magdalene. When Jesus saw his mother, and the disciple whom he loved standing near, he said to his mother, 'Woman, behold, your son!' Then he said to the disciple, 'Behold, your mother!' And from that hour the disciple took her to his own home" (Jn 19:25–27). Mary loves us and wants to keep us close to her Son, and she will help us keep faith in even the darkest times.

Finally, let's take a moment to consider the incredible imagery from Revelation 21, which connects closely with Psalm 51, as theologian Peter Kreeft writes:

> There is a famous painting of Jesus knocking at our door, the door of our hearts and lives. There is no knob on the outside of the door. The knob is on the inside. Jesus does not ignore our free will and knock the door down. The door has to be opened from the inside, by us. Our part is to let the doctor in. His part is to give

> us a healing operation, a heart transplant. The Psalmist prays, "A clean heart create for me, O God" (Ps 51:12). Only God can create something radically new. And we need a new heart. Our fallen and foolish and selfish hearts would not be able to endure God's heaven, God's full presence. And clearly, we can't perform heart surgery on ourselves. Only God can do that work. But he won't do it without our consent. ... At the end of the book of Revelation, Jesus says, "Behold, I make all things new" (Rv 21:5). The first thing he makes new is our hearts, our souls, our selves. And the first beginning, the root of all subsequent growth, is faith.

How blessed we are to have a God so passionately in love with us, that he not only gave his only begotten Son to save us, but continues, every second of every day, to provide every grace and blessing we need to fulfill his desire for us to be with him in heaven — forever. I pray you have gleaned many ways to recognize his healing presence in your life and have already begun to live the abundant life Jesus came to make available to us!

An Invitation to Share

Are you a chicken when it comes to the Sacrament of Reconciliation? What are some things you can do to help you better prepare for the sacrament, that may take away some of the anxiety and help ensure you avail yourself of the healing Jesus wants to give you?

Jeremiah 29:11 often appears on graduation cards and inspirational merchandise. "For I know the plans I have for you, says the LORD, plans for welfare and not for evil, to give you a future and a hope." How can these words of comfort speak to your heart and help you keep believing, even through illness, trial, and tribulation, that God indeed has a plan for your life?

What have you learned about the Sacrament of the Anointing of the Sick after reading this chapter? Does seeing its incredible value to everyone, not just those on their deathbed, give you a new understanding or appreciation for the sacrament? Will you approach it differently now that you've studied it a bit further?

Closing Prayer

Jesus, continue the good work you have begun in me in this final chapter on your mystical and healing presence in the sacraments. You are good and gracious, and I thank you so much for this time spent learning about the great gifts you have abundantly prepared for me. How lavish are your gifts and kindness! I am continually showered by your mercy, love, joy, hope, grace, and so many other blessings that fall all around me while I remain unaware.

Lord, I have seen in every healing story how much you truly love your brothers and sisters. Even in the lessons that frightened or perplexed me, or those times when healing did not come as I'd hoped, you gave me greater hope for heaven, and you showed me that your grace is still abundant; we just need to ask for it. In every word of prayer, I know I will find you. I know you will guide me in every line of Scripture, for "the word of God is living and active, sharper than any two-edged sword, piercing to the division of soul and spirit, of joints and marrow, and discerning the thoughts and intentions of the heart" (Heb 4:12). In every sacrament I am privileged to participate in, I have come to know and believe that

I encounter you there, and I will never be the same because you are there.

Sacred and merciful heart of Jesus, I trust in you. Shower your healing love upon me and all whom I love, according to your Father's perfect will. Amen.

Epilogue

Do you struggle to hear Jesus? Maybe you could try fasting from the noise of the world — perhaps foregoing the morning news, turning off the music in the car, or cutting out some of your TV time. Just fifteen minutes a day will make a difference, and the more time you give to the Lord, the more time you will want to make for the Lord. God is found in the quiet whisper, but we only detect that when we embrace silence. As we read in 1 Kings:

> And he said, "Go forth, and stand upon the mount before the Lord." And behold, the Lord passed by, and a great and strong wind tore the mountains, and broke in pieces the rocks before the Lord, but the Lord was not in the wind; and after the wind an earthquake, but the Lord was not in the earthquake; and after the earthquake a fire, but the Lord was not in the fire; and after the fire a still small voice. (19:11–13)

Another way the Lord speaks to us is through his word, the Scriptures. My morning prayer time always includes the Bible. After reading in Proverbs, "Be attentive to my words; incline your ear to my sayings. Let them not escape from your sight; keep them within your heart. For they are life to him who finds them, and healing to all his flesh. Keep your heart with all vigilance; for from it flow the springs of life" (4:20–23), I started looking for ways to keep God's "word in my heart" (Ps 119:11). Here are a few of my favorite methods:

- Find a verse that also corresponds with a time on the clock. For instance, John 3:16, "For God so loved the world that he gave his only-begotten Son …" Now, when I see that time on the clock, I am automatically drawn into a moment of prayer as I remember the verse. This is especially helpful with verses that remind me not to be afraid and to trust in God!
- For years I would write verses on index cards and stick them all over the place — on the refrigerator, on my car dashboard, on the mirror in the bathroom, on my computer screen, etc. This practice was particularly useful when I was trying to memorize a new Scripture passage!
- Read the daily Mass readings. You can visit the USCCB website, subscribe to one of the many monthly magazines with the readings (some have reflections as well), or sign up for an email from one of the many ministries that offer a daily reflection, such as CatholicMom.com or FamilyRosary.org.

Through my inspirational speaking opportunities, I get to meet the most remarkable people. One such lady was aptly named Grace. At ninety-nine years of age, she holds the record for the oldest attendee to any event I've been blessed to direct. Grace was so feisty and endearing! She was also impeccably dressed in her finest matching purple outfit, complete with chunky fashionable jewelry, on-point pink lipstick, and perfectly coifed hair. I had to ask her the burning question on everyone's mind: What was her secret not only to this long life, but to her health, sharp wit, sense of humor, and joy? Without missing a beat, she presented her five keys for how she reached ninety-nine (and, God-willing, beyond):

- Act young.

- Dress young.
- Dance often.
- Laugh out loud.
- And most importantly, stay close to Jesus!

Amen, Grace. Amen!

In addition to Grace's five keys for a long, joy-filled life, I've added a few of my own that are important for me, especially these two: Take a thirty-minute walk at least five times a week and start every day enjoying coffee with Christ. How about you? What would you add to Grace's inspiring list?

Works Cited

Bergsma, John. *The Word of the Lord: Reflections on the Sunday Mass Readings for Year B*. Emmaus Road Publishing, 2015, 552.

Catechism of the Catholic Church. 2nd ed. Libreria Editrice Vaticana, 1997.

Gribble, Richard, CSC. *Who Do You Say that I Am? Exploring the Question of Christ*. Paulist Press, 2014, 44.

Hahn, Scott, and Curtis Mitch. *Job*. Ignatius Catholic Study Bible. Ignatius Press, 2014, 27.

Kreeft, Peter. *Food for the Soul: Reflections on the Mass Readings (Cycle A)*. Ignatius Press, 2020, 52, 265.

Kreeft, Peter. *Food for the Soul: Reflections on the Mass Readings (Cycle B)*. Ignatius Press, 2021, 252.

Mitch, Curtis, and Edward Sri. *The Gospel of Matthew. Catholic Commentary on Sacred Scripture*. Baker Academic, 2010, 136.

Peyton, Patrick. *All for Her*. Ignatius Press, 2001, 83, 78. Patrick Peyton quotes not attributed to *All for Her* taken from the Archives of Holy Cross Family Ministries, North Easton, MA.

United States Conference of Catholic Bishops. *United States Catholic Catechism for Adults*. USCCB Publishing, 2006, 3773.

About the Author

Drawing from the richness of everyday life, Allison Gingras, visit ReconciledToYou.com, weaves relatable stories, candid honesty, and a touch of humor to share her love of Jesus and the beauty of the Catholic Faith. Fun Allison facts include being obsessed with squirrels, a fanatic of all forms of auto racing, and still able to twirl two batons at once!

She has been a Catholic social media and digital specialist for over fifteen years, having worked for the Catholic Marketing Network, Women in the New Evangelization (WINE), and the Fall River diocese. Allison is currently the director of digital evangelization for Family Rosary USA (and Catholic Mom), part of Holy Cross Family Ministries, continuing the work of Venerable Patrick Peyton, known to many as the "Rosary Priest."

Allison has written six books and is blessed to have contributed to five others. She developed the *Stay Connected Journals for Catholic Women* series with OSV, including her volumes *The Gift of Invitation: 7 Ways Jesus Invites You to a Life of Grace* and *Seeking Peace: A Spiritual Journey from Worry to Trust*. Her numerous book contributions include *Our Friend Faustina* (Marian Press) and the CPA award-winning titles *The Ave Prayer Book for Catholic Mothers*, *Called by Name Daily Devotional for Catholic Women*, and the *Living the Word Catholic Women's Bible*. Her book *Encountering Signs of Faith: My Unexpected Journey with Sacramentals, the Saints, and the Abundant Grace of God* tells the amazing story of teaching the Catholic Faith to her adopted daughter, who is profoundly deaf, while rediscovering for herself the Church's deeply rich teachings and traditions.

Allison's new media experience includes *A Seeking Heart* (radio/podcast) and a Blink series on Catholic TV (Boston). She is excited about her new podcast and video projects with Family Rosary. She joyfully lives out her vocation as a deacon's wife (married for thirty-five years) and the mother of two amazing sons, one precious daughter, and one fabulous daughter-in-law.